NUMBERS

THE KEY TO THE UNIVERSE

COUGH! SPLUTTER!

MURDEROUS MATHS

.MURDEROUS MATHS.

JOIN THE MURDEROUS MATHS GANG
FOR MORE FUN, GAMES AND TIPS AT
WWW.murderousmaths.co.uk

Also by Kjartan Poskitt:
The Knowledge: The Gobsmacking Galaxy
Dead Famous: Isaac Newton and his Apple

·MURDEROUS MATHS·

NUMBERS
THE KEY TO THE UNIVERSE

KJARTAN POSKITT

Illustrated by
Philip Reeve

Hippo

To Mrs Patsy Titcombe and Mrs Tessa Le Bars,
two merry dames who won't understand anything
in this book.

Scholastic Children's Books,
Commonwealth House, 1–19 New Oxford Street,
London WC1A 1NU, UK

A division of Scholastic Ltd
London ~ New York ~ Toronto ~ Sydney ~ Auckland
Mexico City ~ New Delhi ~ Hong Kong

Published in the UK by Scholastic Ltd, 2002

Text copyright © Kjartan Poskitt 2002
Illustrations copyright © Philip Reeve 2002

ISBN 0 439 98116 6

Typeset by TW Typesetting, Midsomer Norton, Somerset
Printed and bound in Great Britain by Cox & Wyman Ltd,
Reading, Berkshire

2 4 6 8 10 9 7 5 3 1

The right of Kjartan Poskitt and Philip Reeve to be identified
as the author and illustrator of this work respectively has been
asserted by them in accordance with the Copyright, Designs and
Patents Act, 1988.

CONTENTS

THE BEGINNING OF THE END

The little moon juddered violently. From several million kilometres away the voice came again.

"Turn it up just a teeny bit louder. Ready? OK. Testing, one two, testing, testing…"

Of course the moon couldn't actually hear the noise coming from the mother planet because sound doesn't travel through the vacuum of empty space. It was the disruption to the planet's gravitational field caused by the mountainous sound system that finally ripped the little moon to bits.

"That should do it. OK, let the audience in."

The greatest rock band in the universe were ready to give their very final last farewell concert. Nebulax were preparing to play to every life form that ever had or ever would exist. This caused several problems, the trickiest of which had been calculating the seating capacity.

"New life forms are evolving all the time," said the promoter, Tezza Goldbars, tapping on her calculator. "You could count them for ever and still not get to the end."

"So how many punters are we expecting in total?" asked Shakk, her assistant.

7

"I make it infinity," said Tezza checking the screen. "So how many seats do we need?"

"Infinity punters will need infinity seats," said Tezza. "Obviously."

Now that's a *lot* of seats – but after the entire audience was settled, Shakk came dashing up to Tezza.

"We've got a problem. The singer's mother has just materialized!"

"I never knew she had a mother," said Tezza.

"Well, she has and she's refusing to go on until her mum has a seat."

"But we've already got all of our infinity seats filled by infinity life forms!" gasped Tezza. "You can't have more seats than infinity!"

It was a tight situation. The crowd were getting restless, the band wouldn't play, tempers were hotting up and things were about to turn very ugly. At times like that there's only one thing to say...

HELLO, MURDEROUS MATHS FANS, AND WELCOME TO ANOTHER BRAIN-BENDING BOOK!

I'VE PEELED YOU ANOTHER GRAPE, O MIGHTY POSKITT...

If you want to solve Tezza's problem of trying to fit one more person on to infinity full seats, you'll need to get your head round NUMBERS which just happens to be the most amazing subject in the universe.

INDEED, 1+2 = 3 IS A TRULY AMAZING FACT!

RUBBISH! IF YOU WANT SOME AMAZING FACTS: KING HENRY VIII HAD SIX WIVES, THE FRENCH WORD FOR CHEESE IS FROMAGE AND IF A CRAB BITES YOUR TOES YOUR FOOT WILL BLEED A BIT.

Let's be fair here. Other subjects such as history, French and biology are cute enough, but let's see what happens when we go off in a rocket to a distant galaxy.

HENRY VIII? FROMAGE? CRAB-TOES-FOOT-BLEED?

? ? ?

The aliens have absolutely no idea what these other subjects are about and frankly it's all a bit embarrassing. However, when they struggle to find some way of talking back, you might just hear...

9

So even when you go to places where all other subjects are just petty and useless, you'll always find that Numbers really are the Key to the Universe!

A warning

Some people will find this book strange. It isn't about doing sums or fractions, it's full of stuff to make you go "ooh" and "ah" and even the occasional "uh?". Imagine answering the door to see yourself standing there. What noise would you make?

Well, you'll be making that noise quite a lot as you read this book.

The mystery is that numbers *seem* so straightforward. You just start with 0 and keep adding 1 and soon there's a nice big long line of them. There's just one little problem – where do you stop? The answer is that you don't. Numbers go on for ever, or – as we say in the maths trade – to infinity. We'll see more about infinity later in the book but before we get there, let's have a quick look at the sort of numbers we'll meet on the way. Just like the queue for the showers in a nudist camp they've got nothing to hide ... or have they?

Here are a few of the freaks to start us off:

- There's a positive whole number that you can add to 1,000,000 and you get an answer that's *bigger* than if you multiply it by 1,000,000. Can you guess what it is? Here's a clue – it's the one that starts all the others!

- $19 = 1 \times 9 + 1 + 9$ and $29 = 2 \times 9 + 2 + 9$. This also works for 39, 49, 59, 69, 79, 89 and 99.

- Did you know that the number 6 is described as *perfect*? We'll find out why it's so gorgeous later on, and also why it encouraged people to spend thousands of years looking for the number 33,550,336.

- If you multiply 21,978 by 4 it turns backwards.

THAT MUST BE THE MOST USELESS FACT IN MATHS!

Oh no it isn't! If you want a *really* useless fact, how about this:

There are 12,988,816 different ways to cover a chessboard with 32 dominoes. (Go on, give it a try! Get a chessboard and 32 dominoes. Each domino should cover two squares or if you haven't got dominoes, you can cut some little paper rectangles out instead.)

Yes – and isn't it brilliant? The good bit is that this book is so full of Pathetically Useless Facts that we've invited some judges in to dish out a few awards.

As you go through the book, be sure to watch out for all the award-winning PUFs as well as the runners up, the merits, the distinctions and so on.

Very nearly, but don't let that put you off having a great time with them. After all, there are loads of people who think they are *so* clever because they can remember every football score for the last 20 years, or the words to every pop song in the charts. But can they do four magic tricks with the number 9?

Who thinks up number facts?

Anyone can have a go at finding newer and stranger number facts (the number "googol" which is a 1 followed by 100 zeros was invented by a nine-year-old), but the experts who spend their whole lives on the subject are called "Pure Mathematicians" and we love them.

These jolly souls spend years agonizing on the meaning of numbers and how they fit together and often their studies are linked with big questions such as "why is the universe here?" and so on. Even if they do have bits of toast stuck to their sleeves and birds nesting in their beards, most of them will happily admit that all their massive brain work is probably a total waste of time. A lot of them are even proud of it. Here's what the great GH Hardy had to say:

> *I have never done anything useful. No discovery of mine has made or is likely to make, directly or indirectly, for good or ill, the least difference to the amenity of the world.*

Poor old Godfrey! He would have been most upset to find that his studies in numbers eventually helped armies to develop mega unbreakable code systems.

Other results from numbers help to explain how the universe started, how curved space works and what the insides of atoms are like. Do you know what wormholes are? If you wanted to travel from our solar system to the nearest star (called Alpha Centauri), it would take nearly $4\frac{1}{2}$ years – even at the speed of light. But scientists now think there is a way of just stepping through a hole in space and getting there immediately. How did they find out about these "wormholes"? By studying numbers!

The strange thing is that numbers on their own mean absolutely nothing. If somebody told you they had just seen eight – you'd have no idea what they were talking about. You can't eat numbers or sit on them or wash them down the plug hole, and yet the more we know about them, the more we realize that our existence relies on them. Who knows – even some of our Pathetically Useless Facts might turn out to be essential one day!

You see? Although this fact seems pathetically useless, it didn't quite qualify. However, if there's only one fact from this book that will stick in your mind for ever, it will probably be this next one because it *must* be one of the most useless statements ever to come from a Pure Mathematician:

FIBONACCI AND THE FOGSWORTH MANOR MIRACLE

High in the attic, Auntie Crystal was stitching together a curious patchwork quilt. As the needle flashed in her bony fingers she smiled for she knew it wasn't just cloth she was piecing together. Elsewhere on the estate the quilt was already working its magic.

Down in the hall, Croak the Butler was aghast.

"Are you really sure about this, madam?" he muttered.

"Absolutely," beamed the Duchess. "I want my guests to feel welcome when they come to the Manor, and this picture of me in the hallway is just the thing."

Croak stepped back and looked at the full-length portrait which featured the Duchess coyly looking over her shoulder. What it didn't feature was any clothes.

"It'll give them a nice surprise when they open the front door," said the Duchess brightly.

"It'll surprise them all right," mumbled Croak as he wondered what on earth had possessed her to record her posterior for posterity.

"A lot of work went into that painting you know," said the Duchess.

"Not to mention a lot of pink paint," muttered Croak to himself.

"Mind you," said the Duchess, "I can't help thinking it's a bit square."

"You mean square as in old-fashioned?" asked Croak, thinking of dusty old pictures in art galleries featuring big Italian ladies lying on couches instead of getting dressed.

"No no," said the Duchess. "It's two metres on each side. Pictures don't look quite right when they're square."

"I could always saw a bit off and make it narrower," said Croak.

"Brilliant!" said the Duchess.

Croak got his saw and laid the picture across the hall table. A few minutes later he held it up.

"It's two metres high and a metre wide now," said Croak.

"Hmmm…" said the Duchess. "It looks a bit too long and thin now. Maybe you should chop the bottom off."

"Good idea," agreed Croak. "The picture would certainly look better without that bottom on it."

"Chop half a metre off the bottom," said the Duchess.

"Oh," said Croak. "In other words you just want me to chop your feet off."

18

"That's it," said the Duchess, but then a few minutes later: "It's better, but now it looks too wide again. Try taking another ten centimetres off each side."

"As you wish," muttered Croak reaching for his saw again. It was going to be a long afternoon...

Meanwhile, Primrose Poppett had been in the garden looking for four-leaf clovers.

"Tell me," she said holding up one single little green clover to her face. "You all seem to have just three leaves. Why is that?"

The little clover didn't say anything, which was very kind, because if it had said anything it would have scared Primrose out of her tiny mind.

"Never mind, I'll find a flower with four petals instead." But after a while she had to remark: "How curious! The iris has three petals, the buttercup has five and as for this rose ... you have eight in the middle and five bigger ones round the outside making 13 altogether. Why do you use such strange numbers?"

The clover nudged the rose but they still said nothing because there are a few rules that plants have to obey. One rule is that your leaves and seeds and petals all have to grow to a fixed mathematical pattern – it doesn't matter whether you're a flower or a clover or even a pineapple or a fir cone. Another rule is that you don't talk to people, because you'll scare them so much that their heads are likely to explode.

"Hey nonny nonny noh," sang Primrose as she put all the flowers in a basket. "I think I'll stick you all in my collecting book and draw little fairies round you. How sweet you'll all look!"

The flowers still said nothing, but boy, it was tempting. Very tempting.

Meanwhile, over by the carrot patch, the language was not quite as soppy.

"Blistering blast and bother!" blurted the Colonel. "These confounded rabbits get everywhere!"

"Sorry old chap," said Rodney Bounder as he emerged from the potting shed. "I just thought a rabbit farm might boost my fortunes a bit."

"Yes, rather a wizard wheeze of mine actually," said Rodney. "I'd got a bit slim in the wallet department, so I decided to get myself a couple of rabbits."

"A couple?" moaned the Colonel. "There's hundreds of the things all eating my veggies!"

"That's the clever bit," said Rodney, checking his notebook. "Rabbits like to get things moving on the baby front as it were so I've been keeping track. In December I just started with the one pair."

"And they produced lots of babies, I suppose," said the Colonel.

"No, in fact I was a bit worried at first," said Rodney. "It seems these rabbits don't produce any babies in their first month, so I didn't get any in January. However, they produced a pair in the second month which was February, then produced another new pair every month after that."

"And I suppose these new pairs of rabbits make more rabbits," said the Colonel.

"Not for the first month, but then they do for every month after that," agreed Rodney. "Here's my progress chart."

"It's quite simple," said Rodney. "The blobs mark each new pair of rabbits. The first pair of rabbits are at the top. They produced a new pair from February onwards. The second pair of rabbits started producing new pairs from April. If you follow the lines you can see how each pair produced more pairs. At the end of each month I counted up the new pairs of rabbits and then added them to the total. For instance, at the end of May I had eight pairs. I got five new pairs in June, so at the end of June I had $8 + 5 = 13$ pairs in total."

"But how do you know the September number?" asked the Colonel. "We haven't got there yet, and besides you haven't drawn it all in."

"I found a short cut," said Rodney. "To work out what I'll have at the end of any month, I just add up the totals for the two months before. If you look at July I finished with 21 pairs in all – which is the total of May and June added together."

"How does that come about?" asked the Colonel.

"Simple," said Rodney. "Look at the end of June, you'll see I had 13 pairs. When I got to the end of July I still had all those 13 pairs *plus* however many new pairs were born in July," said Rodney.

"That's the clever bit!" said Rodney. "I knew that I would get a new pair of rabbits from every pair that was at least two months old. In other words, any pair that were around in May would be producing in July."

"So the number of *new* pairs in July is the same as the May total," said the Colonel feeling rather clever.

22

"You've got it!" said Rodney, "So add the end of May total to the end of June total and you get the end of July total.

"Does that work for every month?" asked the Colonel suspiciously.

"It certainly does," said Rodney. "What's more, I'm just about to calculate how many rabbits I'll have by the Christmas after next!"

DEC	JAN	FEB	MAR	APR	MAY	JUN	JUL	AUG
1	1	2	3	5	8	13	21	34

SEP	OCT	NOV	DEC	JAN	FEB	MAR	APR
55	89	144	233	377	610	987	1597

MAY	JUN	JUL	AUG	SEP	OCT	NOV	DEC
2584	4181	6765	10946	17711	28657	46368	?

"All I do is add October and November together," said Rodney and with a piece of chalk he scribbled on the potting shed wall: 28657 + 46368 = 75025.

"You mean you'll have seventy-five thousand and twenty-five rabbits all eating my carrots?" gasped the Colonel.

"Er ... no," said Rodney.

"Glad to hear it," said the Colonel.

"Actually it's seventy-five thousand and twenty-five *pairs* of rabbits!"

The Colonel was still steaming later that evening when the whole family were gathered in the library to admire the quilt.

"What an interesting pattern, Auntie," said Primrose. "It's all squares getting bigger and bigger."

"I started with the two little squares in the middle," said Auntie Crystal. "Then I added a bigger square to go along the side. Then I put an even bigger square along the next side and so on."

"What do the numbers mean?" asked Rodney.

"That's how big the sides of each square are," chuckled Auntie Crystal. "But surely these numbers are familiar to you?"

"I see there's a square with number three," noticed Primrose. "Then there's a five, an eight and then a thirteen … golly! It's like the petals on my flowers."

"Great gussets!" exclaimed the Colonel. "And it's like those blasted rabbits. He only had one pair for a couple of months, then he had two pairs, then three, then five…"

"…then I had eight, then thirteen!" gasped Rodney. "It's amazing!"

Only the Duchess was silent.

"You're looking left out, dear," said Auntie Crystal.

"I haven't been doing any numbers today," admitted the Duchess. "So your quilt can't have affected me."

"But look at the shape of it!" chuckled Auntie Crystal.

"You're right!" gasped the Duchess. "The shape of your quilt and my picture are almost identical!"

"But how does the quilt work?" they all asked.

"Here's your answer!" said Auntie Crystal and pointed to this sign stitched on the bottom of the quilt:

The golden ratio and the perfect rectangle

This sign is called "phi" and is used to represent a very special number, which has been called the golden ratio, the golden section and the divine proportion:

$$\Phi = 1 \cdot 61803398874989484820458683436 56\ldots$$

Phew! That would take a bit of remembering but there's a formula for it:

$$\Phi = \frac{\sqrt{5} + 1}{2}$$

Try making Φ on your calculator by pushing: 5 $\sqrt{} + 1 \div 2 =$

Phi has a couple of nifty little tricks. To square it you just add 1, and to get the reciprocal (in other words to make it into a fraction) you just subtract 1:

$\Phi^2 = \Phi + 1$ and $1/\Phi = \Phi - 1$

With numbers it looks like this:

$1{\cdot}6180339887 \times 1{\cdot}6180339887 = 2{\cdot}6180339887$

and $1 \div 1{\cdot}6180339887 = 0{\cdot}6180339887$

Make Φ on your calculator and then square it by just pushing $\times$ = (or you can push the x^2 button if you have one). Did you see the difference? If your calculator has a 1/x button you can also try making Φ and then pushing 1/x. (Sometimes you can just push $\div$ = to get the same thing.)

But why is it called the "golden ratio"? For thousands of years people have been making and drawing rectangles of all shapes and sizes, and ages ago they realized that there was a particular shape that they liked best. It wasn't too short and fat and it wasn't too long and skinny. See which of these rectangles you'd pick as your favourite. Do you agree with our panel of experts?

Of course it's all a matter of personal taste, but generally they all agreed that "c" was the *perfect*

rectangle. You'll find that if you measured the long side and divided it by the short side, you'd get the golden ratio Φ. Incidentally this book is almost the perfect shape but it's just a bit too fat.

This Golden Ratio turns up in other shapes too. Pythagoras and his pals were very keen on the "pentagram" or five-pointed star:

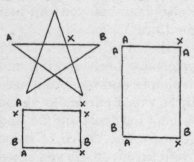

If you copied the line AX twice and also copied the line XB twice, you could put them together to make a perfect rectangle. You could make a bigger perfect rectangle using two AB's and two AX's.

Here's the easy way to draw a perfect rectangle:

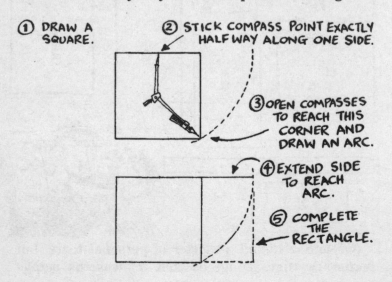

① DRAW A SQUARE.

② STICK COMPASS POINT EXACTLY HALF WAY ALONG ONE SIDE.

③ OPEN COMPASSES TO REACH THIS CORNER AND DRAW AN ARC.

④ EXTEND SIDE TO REACH ARC.

⑤ COMPLETE THE RECTANGLE.

The big rectangle is a perfect rectangle, but if you chop off the square you started with, the small rectangle is also a perfect rectangle.

You can even *fold* a perfect rectangle from a long strip of paper:

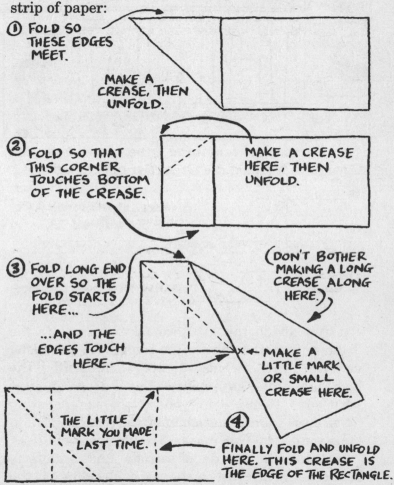

① FOLD SO THESE EDGES MEET.

MAKE A CREASE, THEN UNFOLD.

② FOLD SO THAT THIS CORNER TOUCHES BOTTOM OF THE CREASE.

MAKE A CREASE HERE, THEN UNFOLD.

③ FOLD LONG END OVER SO THE FOLD STARTS HERE...

...AND THE EDGES TOUCH HERE.

(DON'T BOTHER MAKING A LONG CREASE ALONG HERE.)

X ← MAKE A LITTLE MARK OR SMALL CREASE HERE.

THE LITTLE MARK YOU MADE LAST TIME.

④ FINALLY FOLD AND UNFOLD HERE. THIS CREASE IS THE EDGE OF THE RECTANGLE.

All sorts of famous pictures and buildings use the perfect rectangle shape because it just *looks* right.

Here's how the Parthenon at Athens would have looked when it was first built.

If you're not convinced, then see how the Egyptians designed the Great Pyramid at Giza:

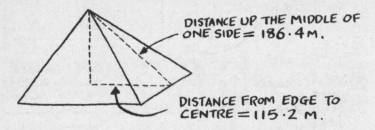

If you divide the distance up the side by the distance from the edge to the centre you get: 186·4 metres ÷ 115·2 metres = 1·618. Incidentally, the Egyptians didn't have metres, but it doesn't matter what you measure it in, you get the same answer. (Even if you were feeling a bit nutty and measured it in miles you'd get 0·1158 miles ÷ 0·07159 miles = 1·618.)

Just like thousands of artists and architects before her, when the Duchess was deciding on the perfect shape for her picture, she found herself gradually making a perfect rectangle. If she had measured the long side and divided it by the short side, she'd have got something near 1·618. But what have the rabbits got to do with it?

The Fibonacci series
Leonardo Fibonacci was living in the Italian town of Pisa about 800 years ago when the famous Straight Up Tower of Pisa was being built. As fate would have it, two curious things happened around the same time. The tower started leaning and Leonardo developed his famous series of numbers which goes like this:

As we've seen with the rabbits, to get the next number in the series you just add the last two numbers together. The numbers are also the sizes of the squares on Auntie Crystal's quilt. But why should the quilt be the same shape as the Duchess's picture?

Fibonacci's series does lots of strange things and one of them is that it conjures up the number Φ, which you'll remember is about equal to 1·618. What we do is take two numbers next to each other in the series and divide the bigger one by the smaller one. We'll start at the beginning with the two ones and move along to see what we get:

31

1/1 = 1 which is quite a lot *less* than 1·618.

2/1 = 2 which is a bit *more* than 1·618.

3/2 = 1·5 which is *less* than 1·618 but getting a bit closer.

5/3 = 1·667 which is *more* than 1·618 but getting even closer.

8/5 = 1·6 which is just a tiny bit *less* than 1·618.

13/8 = 1·625 which is an even teenier bit *more* than 1·618.

21/13 = 1·615 which is a teeny-weeny bit *less* than 1·618.

34/21 = 1·619 ... oh COME ON!

How close do you want it to be before you're convinced? To save time we'll grab two of the biggest numbers off Rodney's rabbit chart and see how close they come to making Φ:

46368/28657 = 1·6180339882

NOT BAD, BUT THAT 2 SHOULD BE A 7.

The sides of Auntie Crystal's quilt are 55 and 34, so the ratio is 55/34 which is 1·617647. This makes it almost identical in shape to a perfect rectangle, which is what the Duchess had been creating.

How plants count

This is where maths gets really strange.

If you count up the petals on a flower, in most cases you get a Fibonacci number. Roses are especially interesting because a wild rose has five petals, but a neat looking normal rose has five petals around the outside, and a tighter cluster of eight petals in the middle. Occasionally you'll find buttercups with six petals but that's because they started with three big petals each of which divided into two. Even daisies try their best and have either 55 or 89 petals – although to be fair they sometimes lose count and have a few petals more or less.

Of course, there are lots of plants that don't seem to obey the rules, but that's often because they are mutants or hybrids that have been created artificially, or plants that have been tampered with while they were growing. However, if you have a tall sunflower that's been in the same pot since it was a seed, check to see if all the leaves come off the stem at different heights. If they do then you should find something interesting.

Find a leaf low down and imagine tying a thread to it. Then imagine tying the thread to the next leaf above it, and then the next one and the next working the thread around the stem the shortest way each time. If you count the bottom leaf as 0, then the *fifth* leaf you get to should be directly above it. You'll also find your thread goes around the stem *two* times.

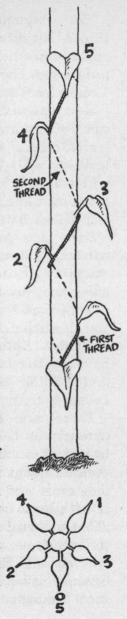

33

Now imagine linking the leaves with a second thread, but this time it goes round the stem in the opposite direction. You'll find it goes around the stem *three* times. Look at the numbers we've got: 2, 3, 5. These come next to each other in the Fibonacci series!

Next time you're in a big garden or a park, see if you can spot any other plants that have a long stem with leaves coming off it. There are lots that produce leaves on a 1-1-2 system, but you might find a plant with a 2-3-5 or even a 3-5-8 system. In other words, if you start at a bottom leaf and count up, the *eighth* leaf you reach will be directly above your starting leaf.

Something that's a bit harder to spot are spiral patterns. The seeds in the head of a sunflower are set in two patterns of spirals, usually 34 spirals going one way and 55 the other. (A big sunflower might have 55 spirals one way and 89 the other!) If you think that would be murderous to count, then what about little daisy heads? They are supposed to have a pattern of 21 spirals one way and 34 the other, but imagine Leonardo trying to count them...

There are Fibonacci spiral patterns in the heads of lots of other flowers, and even on things like leaves, pine cones and pineapples. If you want to find out more about this visit *www.murderousmaths.co.uk*, but in the meantime, here's something a lot easier to see for yourself: How many ridges are there on a banana? (Clue: it's a Fibonacci number... or a squashed banana.)

34

The nautilus

Suppose that before you were born you had already decided you wanted to be famous all over the world. The system works something like this:

The nautilus grows to about 25 cm long and it's a massive star because as its shell develops it creates one of the most fascinating shapes in maths. Sure, common snails and other creatures try their best but they don't get their names and pictures in posh maths books.

WE INTERRUPT THIS BOOK TO BRING YOU PAGE 37 AND SOME FACTS ABOUT THIS STRANGE NUMBER.

- A silly trick: pick any number from 1 to 9. Multiply by 3 then 37. What do you get?
- A sillier trick: grab a calculator and push any number from 1 to 9. Then push $\times 3 \times 7 \times 11 \times 13 \times 37 =$ Satisfying, isn't it?
- Pick any number between 3 and 27. Multiply it by 37 and you get a 3 digit answer. Obviously this answer will divide exactly by 37, but the funny thing is that if you move the first digit of the answer to the end, *or* you move the last digit to the front, the results will also divide exactly by 37 (e.g. $37 \times 17 = 629$). You'll find that 296 and 962 both divide exactly by 37 too.
- Your body temperature should be 37° Celsius.
- Pick any number, square the digits and add them. Do it again and again and again. You'll either end up with 1 or you'll end up with a sequence that goes 37-58- 89-145-42-20-4-16-37.
- Finally: $1 \div 37 = 0 \cdot 027027027\ldots$
  and $1 \div 27 = 0 \cdot 037037037\ldots$

THERE. WE HOPE YOU ENJOYED PAGE 37 AND WE'LL NOW RETURN YOU TO THE REST OF THE BOOK.

Where were we? Ah, yes... Let's have one last look at the pattern on Auntie Crystal's quilt:

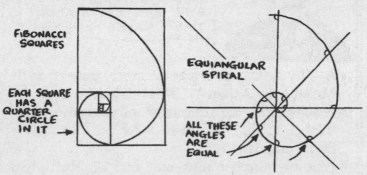

FIBONACCI SQUARES

EACH SQUARE HAS A QUARTER CIRCLE IN IT →

EQUIANGULAR SPIRAL

ALL THESE ANGLES ARE EQUAL

If you mark a quarter circle in each square you get a spiral shape. This shape is very close to the shape of an "equiangular" spiral, and this is also the shape produced by the humble nautilus. There's just one bad bit of news about this. If you're a nautilus and you see a mathematician in a diving suit heading your way, then quick – disguise yourself. Otherwise...

LOOK AT THAT PERFECT EQUIANGULAR SPIRAL!

CHOP!

BLURK!

Fibonacci fun

Here's a surprising experiment. Imagine you've got a massive sack of 1p and 2p pieces and you're feeding them into your piggy bank.

● If you want to put 1p in your piggy bank, there's only *one* way to do it. You just put in a single 1p coin.

- If you want to put 2p in, there are *two* ways to do it. You can either put in two 1p coins or one 2p coin.
- If you want to put 3p in, there are *three* ways to do it. You can put in three 1p coins, or a 2p then a 1p or a 1p then a 2p.
- If you want to put 4p or 5p in, have a look at this list:

AMOUNT TO PUT IN	NUMBER OF WAYS	DIFFERENT WAYS
1p	1	①
2p	2	①+① ②
3p	3	①+①+① ②+① ①+②
4p	5	①+①+①+① ②+①+① ①+②+① ①+①+② ②+②
5p	8	①+①+①+①+① ②+①+①+① ①+②+①+① ①+①+②+① ①+①+①+② ②+②+① ②+①+② ①+②+②

(I'M STUFFED!)

Now that you've found out about the Fibonacci series, have a guess how many ways there are of putting in 6p, then check your answer by trying to write all the different ways out like we've done here. If you manage to find them all, try the experiment with 7p or 8p or bigger amounts! See how you rate:

FINDING ALL THE WAYS FOR 6p	FINDING ALL THE WAYS FOR 7p	FINDING ALL THE WAYS FOR 8p	FINDING ALL THE WAYS FOR £132·61
PRETTY CLEVER	STUNNINGLY CLEVER	DROP DEAD GORGEOUSLY CLEVER	SEEK HELP URGENTLY

The fabulous Fibonacci trick

Murderous Maths fans can make a trick out of almost anything, and good old Fibonacci doesn't let us down. Get a friend to do this:

- Draw out a set of 6 boxes and number them 1–6.
- Pick *any* two numbers between 1 and 9 (or you can use higher numbers if you feel clever) and write them in boxes 1 and 2.
- Add boxes 1 + 2 and write the answer in box 3.
- Next add boxes 2 + 3 and put the answer in box 4.
- Add 3 + 4 and fill in box 5
  At this point you write a number on another piece of paper!
- Add boxes 4 + 5 to fill in box 6.
- Finally add up the total of all six boxes…

… but your friend will be gobsmacked to see that you have *already written* the answer down before box 6 was even filled in!

THE SECRET: All you do is look at the number in box 5 and multiply it by 4 and write it down!

Here's an example:

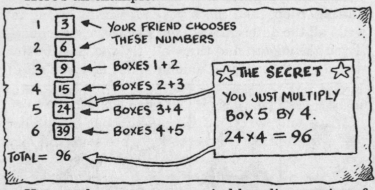

1	3	← YOUR FRIEND CHOOSES
2	6	← THESE NUMBERS
3	9	← BOXES 1 + 2
4	15	← BOXES 2 + 3
5	24	← BOXES 3 + 4
6	39	← BOXES 4 + 5
TOTAL = 96		←

☆ THE SECRET ☆
YOU JUST MULTIPLY
BOX 5 BY 4.
24 × 4 = 96

You can do an even more mind-boggling version of this same trick by drawing out 10 boxes to start with.

Your friend chooses any two numbers to go in the first two boxes, then fills in all the other boxes and then adds them ALL up as before. You can write down the final answer by looking at box 7 and multiplying it by 11.

(Do you know how to multiply a two digit number by 11 quickly? Add the digits and put the answer in the middle. $23 \times 11 = 253$ because $2 + 3$ makes 5 and that goes in the middle. $79 \times 11 = 869$ because $7 + 9 = 16$ and you put the 6 in the middle and add the "1" to the 7.)

$1 \div 89 = 0.0112359550561797...$

And here's something very strange to finish with! Write out the Fibonacci sequence (starting with 0) with the units of each number in a diagonal, and then add them up.

We've only written the sequence out to number 144 here, and as soon as the sequence stops the very last few digits will be wrong. But if we kept going you'd get all the decimal digits of $1 \div 89$!

SQUARES, TRIANGLES, CUBES AND WHAT THEY GET UP TO TOGETHER

Do you remember when you were just starting out with maths? The first thing you learnt to do was count to 10 and once you'd done it you thought you were just brilliant. And why not? You could answer any tough question they threw at you, such as "what comes after three?" A well-paid career as an international financier was yours for the asking.

But then it got murderous. Your great talent was noticed by some huge person who was a whole year older than you and was big enough to sit on the toilet without falling in. This person would invent completely impossible questions such as "what does five take away two make?" Gulp! The only way to crack such a devastating mathematical enigma was to reach for the counters. You laid out five counters, then took away two. You counted up the others and in well under an hour you had the answer ... three.

Eventually the time came when you grew out of using counters. You learnt to work out sums using calculators, computers or (most impressive) a pencil and paper. You've probably forgotten that you ever used counters and by now they are scattered all around the place. Under flower pots, down the back of the armchair, on top of the wardrobe, inside the cat... WELL GO AND GET THEM!

GOT 'EM!

Counters have the power to explain things in a way that calculators and computers can never do. You're going to be amazed at what they can tell you, and how they can help you avoid some truly diabolical sums.

Squares

You probably know that square numbers come from multiplying a number by itself, and we show that by writing a little "2" after the number. So if somebody asks you what "three squared" is, you can dazzle them by writing $3^2 = 3 \times 3 = 9$. This shows us that 9 is the *square* of 3. You can also do these sums *backwards* and there are three ways of asking the same question depending on how bright you are:

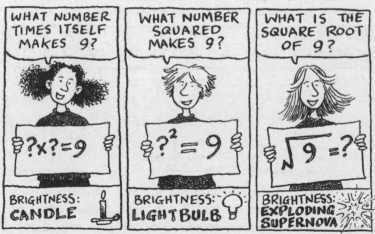

You'll notice there's a special sign for square roots which is like a big zigzag tick and for some strange reason it's rather satisfying to draw. Probably because if you do it fast it feels a bit like signing your autograph.

Calculator tips: You can usually get "squares" on your calculator quickly just by pushing " × = " So for 18² you push 18 × = and you should get 324. Getting square roots is pretty miserable unless you've got a "√" button.

It's playtime...

People call square numbers "squares" for short and the fun bit is you can draw out squares by using counters like this:

Here's a square with 3 counters along each side and you get 9 counters in total. All very obvious, but now let's write out the numbers 0 to 10 with their squares written underneath. Notice what the last digit of each square is!

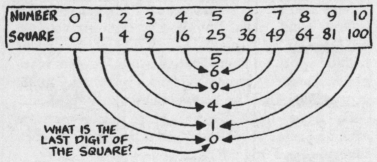

NUMBER	0	1	2	3	4	5	6	7	8	9	10
SQUARE	0	1	4	9	16	25	36	49	64	81	100

WHAT IS THE LAST DIGIT OF THE SQUARE?

The last digit changes in a fixed pattern which goes 0-1-4-9-6-5-6-9-4-1-0. If you write out the squares of numbers from 10 to 20 you get exactly the same pattern!

NUMBER	10	11	12	13	14	15	16	17	18	19	20
SQUARE	100	121	144	169	196	225	256	289	324	361	400

This pattern always works because the last digit of a square only depends on the last digit of the number you're squaring. So...

THE NUMBER YOU'RE SQUARING ENDS IN:	THE ANSWER MUST END IN:
0	00
1	1
2	4
3	9
4	6
5	25
6	6
7	9
8	4
9	1

Suppose somebody told you to work out $578,908^2$ in your head. Urgh! But there's one thing you can tell them straight away – the last digit of the answer has to be a 4. Numbers that end in 5 are even more exciting because if somebody asks you what $74,995^2$ is, you know that the last *two* digits have to be 25.

The creepy bit is that even little plastic counters with no brains at all realize that they have to obey this rule, so if this happens...

I'VE JUST MADE A SQUARE WITH 718 COUNTERS.

...you know she's lying because the counters wouldn't let a square end with an 8.

Making bigger squares

First let's make a 3×3 square which will need 9 counters. Now we'll turn it into a 4×4 square: how many extra counters do we need?

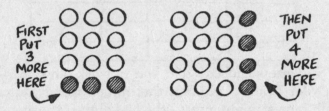

First we put 3 counters along the bottom to make a rectangle. Then we put 4 counters up the side to complete the 4×4 square. The total of extra counters we needed was $3 + 4 = 7$. Altogether in our 4×4 square we've got 16 counters.

That's how it works with counters, and this is how it works with sums: $3^2 + 3 + 4 = 4^2$. The good bit is that this always works – it doesn't matter what size of square you start with. If you started with a 9×9 square of counters you'd find that: $9^2 + 9 + 10 = 10^2$.

You can check this yourself either by doing the sums or by putting out loads of counters. This leads to some nifty short cuts as our judging panel will demonstrate...

You can see why it's a handy short cut. It would have been expecting a lot for a dog to work out 218×218, wouldn't it?

The difference of differences

The amount you have to add on to one square to get the next one is called the "difference" between them. For instance the difference between 25 and 36 is 11. Have a look at how the differences get bigger:

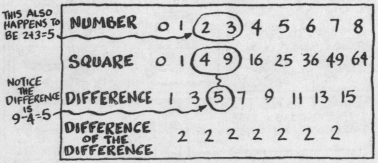

THIS ALSO HAPPENS TO BE 2+3=5

NOTICE THE DIFFERENCE IS 9-4=5

NUMBER	0	1	2	3	4	5	6	7	8
SQUARE	0	1	4	9	16	25	36	49	64
DIFFERENCE		1	3	5	7	9	11	13	15
DIFFERENCE OF THE DIFFERENCE			2	2	2	2	2	2	2

See how the differences are all the odd numbers going up in order? As each odd number is 2 bigger than the last one, you can say that the difference of the difference is 2 each time, and it doesn't matter how big your squares get!

In Fogsworth Manor they are planning to make a square sun terrace with square slabs.

"Thirty-five years ago we had a terrace with 1,369 square slabs," said the Colonel. "And we arranged

them to make a big perfect square. It was such a pity that Auntie did that wheely in her traction engine and smashed them to dust."

"Then 18 years ago we made the new terrace," said the Duchess. "It had an extra row of slabs along the North and East sides making a slightly bigger square. That terrace used 1,444 slabs in total."

"It was just rotten luck that giant elephant mole burrowed its way up through the centre and smashed it all to bits," said the Colonel.

"Let's try once more," said the Duchess. "And this time we'll make the square slightly bigger again."

"How many slabs would we need for the new square?" asked the Colonel.

"It would help if we knew how many slabs we had along each side of the old square," said the Duchess. "But how do we work that out?"

"Aha!" said the Colonel proudly. "I've got just the gizmo for that sort of thing! It's the old regimental Calcatronic Wizard. Natty little device, what?"

"What's that smell?" asked the Duchess after the machine was plugged in.

"It's just warming up," said the Colonel. "Now then, the last terrace had 1,444 slabs so we ask it what the square root of 1,444 is, and that'll be the number of slabs we had along each side. Aha – it looks like the answer's nearly here…"

Bzzz kuzink ding BLAMM!

"Oh dear," said the Duchess, stepping back from the smoking crater where the Calcatronic Wizard had been. "If we can't work out how many slabs were along each side, we'll never know how many slabs we need to buy to make the new bigger square."

It's at this point that a bit of murderous maths comes to the rescue. Amazingly enough, we don't need to know how many slabs were along each side of the terrace! All we need to know is that the first square used 1,369 slabs and the next square up used 1,444 slabs. The difference of these two squares is 1444−1369 = 75. As the differences between squares increases by 2 every time, we know that the difference between 1444 and the next square up is 75 + 2 = 77. So the total number of slabs needed for the new square terrace is 1444 + 77 = 1521.

If you get a calculator and test the numbers 1369, 1444 and 1521, they should all be perfect squares!

The difference of two squares

So far we've only increased the size of the square by one. Life gets more curious when you jump from say a 4×4 square to a 7×7 square because it involves one of the coolest tricks in the number world...

> **The difference of two squares is the sum multiplied by the difference.**

Erk! If you've never seen this rule before and think it sounds mad, don't worry, you're not going soft in the head. This is just a very short version of the rule, but if the whole thing was written out clearly it would take half a page so we won't bother. People usually explain this rule using algebra and it would look like this: $x^2-y^2=(x-y)(x+y)$ ... but don't let that put you off! If you've got your counters ready and you can keep a cool head, we might just be able to unravel this minor maths miracle another way.

First we'll see what the rule means with numbers. It starts by saying "The difference of two squares" so let's pick two numbers, make them into squares and see what happens. We'll pick 7 and 4.

● To get *the difference of two squares* we just square them and take the small one from the big one. We get 7^2-4^2. This isn't too bad because $7^2=49$ and $4^2=16$ and then $49-16=33$.

● Now according to the rule this answer should equal the sum of our two numbers (which is $7+4$) multiplied by the difference of the two numbers (which is $7-4$). The sum works out as $7+4=11$ and the difference is $7-4=3$. Therefore when we *multiply the sum by the difference* we get $11\times3=33$.

Both answers are the same so it works! Neat, eh?

The jolly bit is that we can show this with our friendly little counters.

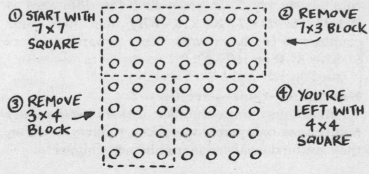

① START WITH 7×7 SQUARE
② REMOVE 7×3 BLOCK
③ REMOVE 3×4 BLOCK
④ YOU'RE LEFT WITH 4×4 SQUARE

We start with 49 counters in the 7×7 square. We remove a block of counters on the top to make the shape just 4 rows high. Then we remove a block up the side to end with the 4×4 square. So how many counters did we take off?

To make it obvious, we'll swing one of the blocks of removed counters around and stick it neatly on to the end of the other one.

All the removed counters together now make one big block which measures $(7+4)$ counters on one side and $(7-4)$ counters on the other side, so the number of counters in the block is $(7+4) \times (7-4)$ counters. To work this sort of thing out you have to do the bits in the brackets first and BINGO we get the same thing as we had before: $11 \times 3 = 33$.

So: we started with 7^2 counters, we took away $(7+4) \times (7-4)$ and were left with 4^2 counters. Or as the rule said: $7^2 - (7+4) \times (7-4) = 4^2$

This rule ALWAYS works! If you used your counters to try $5^2 - 2^2$ you'd find the difference is $(5+2) \times (5-2) = 7 \times 3 = 21$. Why not use your counters to try it out with other squares such as $9^2 - 5^2$ or $8^2 - 6^2$ or $137^2 - 93^2$?

How many squares are there?
There are an *infinite* number of them because any number can be squared to make a square. However, they get further apart as numbers get bigger:

Between 0 and 100 there are 10 squares:
1, 4, 9, 16, 25, 36, 49, 64, 81, 100
Between 101 and 200 there are 4 squares:
121, 144, 169, 196
Between 201 and 300 there are 3 squares:
225, 256, 289
Between 301 and 400 there are 3 squares:
324, 361, 400
Between 401 and 500 there are 2 squares:
441, 484
...and so on.

But even though the high squares are a long way apart, it's amazing how often they just happen to turn up. Try this:

1 Pick any FOUR consecutive numbers and multiply them together (e.g. $23 \times 24 \times 25 \times 26 = 358800$)

2 Add 1 ($358800 + 1 = 358801$)

3 Your answer will be a square!

4 You can tell which square it is. All you do is multiply your biggest and smallest numbers together and add 1. ($23 \times 26 = 598$ then $598 + 1 = 599$ Yes, you'll find that $599^2 = 358801$)

Try it with your own numbers – it always works. Strange but true.

Some useless square facts

- 49 is 7^2. But if you put 48 in the middle you'll get 4489 which is 67^2. And if you put another 48 in the middle you get $444889 = 667^2$ and $44448889 = 6667^2$ and so on.

- If you divide any square number by 8 you get a remainder of 0, 1 or 4.

- You can make any number by adding together four (or less) squares. E.g. $14 = 3^2 + 2^2 + 1^2$ and $39 = 6^2 + 1^2 + 1^2 + 1^2$ and $4,097 = 64^2 + 1^2$ and $4,095 = 63^2 + 10^2 + 5^2 + 1^2$.

- $1^2 = 1$ $11^2 = 121$ $111^2 = 12321$ $1111^2 = 1234321$ $11111^2 = ...$ go on, have a guess!

- $13^2 = 169$ which gives us two facts:
  1 To get 14^2 you just swap the last two digits of the answer round because $14^2 = 196$.
  2 You can write both numbers backwards and get $31^2 = 961$. This works with 12 too because $12^2 = 144$ and $21^2 = 441$.

How to work out 3333333333333^2 in your head at lightning speed

Get a calculator and see what 33^2 comes to. Then work out 333^2. And then work out 3333^2. And then work out 33333^2 and so on ... but by this time you won't need a calculator!

Triangles

If you're using counters, you can make triangles instead of squares like this:

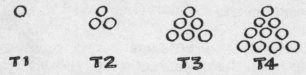

The first triangle only has one counter along each side. It's not much of a triangle really, but you've got to start somewhere. The total number of counters in the first triangle is 1, so we say that *the first triangle number* = 1. As it's a bit dull writing out "the first triangle number" we just shorten it to: T1 = 1.

The second triangle has two counters along each side. The total number of counters in the second triangle is 3, so we say that the *second triangle number* or T2 = 3.

In the same way you'll see that T3 = 6 and T4 = 10.

Suppose we want to turn the fourth triangle into the fifth triangle...

All we need to do is add one more line of 5 counters, and you'll see that T5 = T4 + 5 = 15.

ADD 5 MORE COUNTERS

T5

There's a bit more about triangle numbers in *More Murderous Maths*, but just for now we're going to see something rather good.

How to turn triangles into squares

The list of triangle numbers starts with 1, 3, 6, 10, 15, 21, 28, 36, 45 .... and so on. The amazing thing is that if you take ANY triangle number and multiply it by 8, then add 1, you ALWAYS end up with a square number!

For instance, T4 is 10, so we can take $10 \times 8 = 80$ then add 1 to get 81. And of course $81 = 9^2$. Why does this work?

We can show this by getting the counters out again. Let's start by making the third triangle number with 6 counters...

Super. All we do is push it over a bit and add a second T3 to make a rectangle.

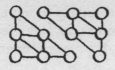

You'll notice the rectangle measures 3×4 counters and the important bit is that it is one counter longer than it is wide. This means that if you put four of these rectangles together you get this...

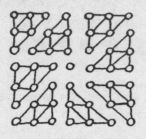

EIGHT TRIANGLES
WITH AN EXTRA
COUNTER IN THE
MIDDLE.

...a square of counters with a gap for one more counter in the middle!

So if we check what we've got, there are 8 T3 triangles in total and one extra counter. This has made a 7×7 square. If you want to check the numbers, there are 6 counters in a T3 triangle so $6 \times 8 = 48$. Adding 1 makes 49 which is 7^2.

You'll see that the third triangle number converted into the *seventh* square number. If you play about with a load of counters you'll find that you can make ANY odd square number out of triangle numbers. Just subtract 1 from the number you want squared and divide by 2. So if you wanted to know which triangle number you could make 11^2 with, you just work out $11 - 1 = 10$ then divide by 2. You'll find the 5th triangle number is the one you want.

Cubes

A cube is what you get when you multiply a number by itself three times, and you can indicate it it with a little "3". For instance $2^3 = 2 \times 2 \times 2 = 8$. (Notice that 2^3 is NOT the same as $2 \times 3 = 6$.)

You can say 8 is the *cube* of 2, or you can say 2 is the *cube root* of 8. You can even make a model of 2^3 if you've got loads of dice or sugar cubes or little cube building bricks...

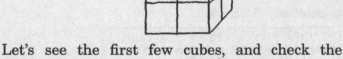

Let's see the first few cubes, and check the differences between them as they get bigger:

NUMBER	0	1	2	3	4	5	6	7
CUBE	0	1	8	27	64	125	216	343
DIFFERENCE		1	7	19	37	61	91	127
DIFFERENCE OF THE DIFFERENCE			6	12	18	24	30	36
DIFFERENCE OF THE DIFFERENCE OF THE DIFFERENCE				6	6	6	6	6

As you'll see, the cube numbers get bigger very quickly. 1^3 is just 1 but by the time you get to 4^3 you've already got to 64. To find out what's going on, we look at the differences between the cubes which are $1 - 7 - 19$ and so on. These get bigger quickly too, so let's look at the differences of the differences! These are $6 - 12 - 18$ ... hey! With a bit of luck you'll realize that these are all the numbers in the 6 times table! That's why the difference of the difference of the difference is always 6.

HAR HAR! DIFFERENCES OF DIFFERENCES IS JUST RUBBISH!

Oh no. Trust Professor Fiendish to crash in and confuse everything. He doesn't realize that this is just a simple way of working out more cubes. If we wanted to work out 8^3 we could do it without having to multiply $8 \times 8 \times 8$.

OH YEAH? WELL HERE'S A CUBE MADE OF SUGAR LUMPS WITH 8 ALONG EACH SIDE. I BET I CAN WORK OUT HOW MANY LUMPS ARE IN IT BEFORE YOU!

Easy. We just look at the end of our list of cubes and put in a few extra numbers. Tum tee tum...

NUMBER		4	5	6	7	8
CUBE		64	125	216	343	☐
DIFFERENCE			61	91	127	☐
DIFFERENCE OF DIFFERENCE				30	36	☐
DIFFERENCE OF DIFFERENCE OF DIFFERENCE					6	6

① PUT A '6' IN HERE BECAUSE THIS LINE IS <u>ALL</u> SIXES

② THIS NUMBER IS 36 + 6 = 42

③ THIS NUMBER IS 127 + 42 = 169

The idea is to fill numbers in the spaces. You start at the bottom because we know all the numbers on this line are 6. The number in the next line up has to be 6 more than the last number (which is 36) so it's 42. Moving up a line we now know that the number we need to put in is $127 + 42 = 169$. Finally we can work out 8^3 by adding $343 + 169$. But let's see how the Professor has been getting on...

Nice to see him working hard. Of course the sum he's trying to do is $8 \times 8 \times 8$ which is a double multiplication, but we're getting the answer just by adding! Let's finish it off: $8^3 = 343 + 169 = 512$. We've done it, Professor! How are you getting on?

A cube fact
153, 370, 371 and 407 all have something in common. Each of them is the "sum of the cubes of their digits". In other words $153 = 1^3 + 5^3 + 3^3$.

Centred hexagons and Grizelda's arrows
Grizelda the Grisly is buying some arrows and she can choose from having just 1 single practice arrow, the Skirmish bundle of 7 arrows, the Raider bundle of 19 arrows or the Big Battle bundle of 37 arrows. (Yes, fans of 37, your favourite number has turned up again!) The next size up is the Invasion bundle and the question is: how many arrows does it contain?

This might seem like a strange sequence of numbers, but what's even stranger is that you've already seen it! Try looking back a few pages – if you can find the sequence, you'll find the answer.

This sequence of numbers is called the "centred hexagonal" numbers which just happens to be a good way of bundling up arrows as neatly as possible. You'll notice that the ends of the bundles look like hexagons:

You start with one arrow, then to make the single arrow into a hexagon, you put 6 arrows round the outside. (If you try this with round counters or lots of 1p pieces, you'll find that 6 of them will go round the centre one exactly.) The next hexagon needs 12 more arrows round the outside, the next one needs 18 more arrows. Each time the number of extra arrows goes up by 6, so to make the Invasion bundle you need 24 extra arrows. The answer is $37 + 24 = 61$. (Did you find this same sequence on page 57? It's the "differences" of the cubes.)

By now you won't be surprised that you can turn triangle numbers into centred hexagons. Just get any triangle number, multiply it by 6 and add 1. For instance T2 is 3 so $3 \times 6 + 1 = 19$. If you've run out of counters you can lay it out with a range of deep-sea creatures and it looks like this:

Triangular pyramids and Urgum's cannonballs
Urgum the Axeman has heard about Grizelda's little shopping trip, so he's been ordering a few spare cannonballs. Cannonballs come in triangular piles shaped like pyramids, so how many balls can he expect in the "Broadside"?

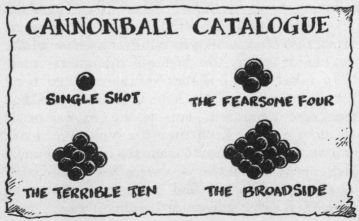

In the piles of cannonballs, each layer is a triangle and so the number of balls in the layer is a triangle number! As ever the first pile has just one ball, and 1 is the first triangle number or T1.

IST LAYER   2ND LAYER   3RD LAYER   4TH LAYER

The second pyramid has two layers which you can see are T1 + T2. So the number of balls in the second pyramid is T1 + T2 = 1 + 3 = 4. The third pyramid is T1 + T2 + T3 = 1 + 3 + 6 = 10.

Therefore the "Broadside", which has four layers in a pyramid, will have T1 + T2 + T3 + T4 balls. This is 1 + 3 + 6 + 10 = 20.

These numbers are called **tetrahedral** and the odd fact is that only three of them are squares. The first tetrahedral number is 1 which is also equal to 1^2. The second tetrahedral number is 4 which is 2^2. But the third tetrahedral number is 10 and the 4th is 20 and the 5th is 35 and the 6th is 56 ... have a guess what the only other square tetrahedral number is? It's the 48th tetrahedral number which just happens to be 19,600 or 140^2. If Urgum wanted a pyramid this big, the bottom layer would be a triangle containing 1,176 cannonballs with 48 along each edge!

Square pyramids and the number 91

If Urgum's cannonballs were arranged in piles with square layers rather than triangles, you'd get a completely different set of numbers. Each layer would be a square number, so the layers would go 1, 4, 9, 16, 25, 36, 49 ... and so on.

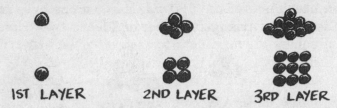

IST LAYER   2ND LAYER   3RD LAYER

The smallest pyramid would be 1, the next would be $1+4=5$ then $1+4+9=14$. Skip on a bit to the 6th square pyramid number and you get:

$1+4+9+16+25+36=91$.

Funnily enough, if you look at the 13th triangle number you get:

$1+2+3+4+5+6+7+8+9+10+11+12+13=91$.

And if you aren't already hot with excitement – Grizelda finally decided to buy the next size up from the "Invasion" bundle. Go on – treat yourself and work out what the next "centred hexagonal number" is and so find out how many arrows were in the "World Domination" bundle!

Squared triangles and cubes

If you write out the triangle numbers, then square them, then work out the differences, look what you get:

NUMBER	0	1	2	3	4	5	6	7
TRIANGLE NUMBER	0	1	3	6	10	15	21	28
TRIANGLE SQUARED	0	1	9	36	100	225	441	784
DIFFERENCES		1	8	27	64	125	216	343

Yes – it's the cubes!

So ... if you multiply a triangle number by 8 and add 1 you always make a square and if you multiply a triangle number by 6 and add 1 you get a centred hexagonal number and if you square two triangle numbers that are next to each other and then find the difference, you'll get a cube. Phew!

As you claw your way through to the end of this chapter, you'd be forgiven for thinking that you'd already suffered from quite enough pathetic facts. If so, then you'd better brace yourself as we proudly deliver a massive double blow to your intelligence...

Two REALLY pitiful useless cube/square facts

- 8 is the only cube that is 1 less than a square. In other words $8+1=9$, which is a square. But if you get ANY other cube such as 125 or 343, when you add 1 you won't get a square.

- $69^2 = 4761$ and $69^3 = 328509$. These two answers use all the digits from 0 to 9 between them. Sixty-nine is the only number that produces this result.

Fermat's Last Theorem

Over 300 years ago, a French official called Pierre de Fermat used to tinker round with all sorts of maths for fun. Quite often he thought of the most amazing and simple answers to huge problems and he had the habit of scribbling these in the margins of books. But there was one problem that  drove everybody completely nutty for years and it was this...

Everyone knew there were an unlimited number of ways in which you could add two squares to make a third square such as:

$3^2 + 4^2 = 5^2$ or $5^2 + 12^2 = 13^2$ and $7^2 + 24^2 = 25^2$.

These are called "Pythagorian triples" and you can work out some more of these yourself:

- Your first number can be ANY odd number. We'll try it out with 13.
- Square it so $13^2 = 169$.
- Subtract 1 so $169 - 1 = 168$.
- Divide the answer by 2 so you get $168 \div 2 = 84$. That's your second number.
- To get the third number just add 1 so $84 + 1 = 85$.
- If you can be bothered to test it, you'll find that $13^2 + 84^2 = 85^2$ and the fun bit is that you got the numbers without working out ugly stuff such as 84^2.

The problem was – could anybody find a similar sum that worked with cubes? In other words, was there a way to make this sum work by filling in the gaps with whole numbers? $(\ )^3 + (\ )^3 = (\ )^3$

In fact, it didn't have to be cubes. Could *anyone* find *any* answer using *any* power such as 4th powers or 5th powers or even... $( )^{247} + ( )^{247} = ( )^{247}$

Everyone tried for hundreds of years to find just one answer that worked, but in the end they decided it must be impossible. The trouble is that no one could actually prove it was impossible ... until along came Pierre who scribbled down the side of a page in a book:

> I "have discovered a "truly marvellous proof which this margin is not large enough to contain."

Yes, Fermat claimed to have shown that for sums like this there wasn't a single answer in the whole universe that would work with cubes, or fourth powers or fifth powers or indeed any other power bigger than 2.

The beauty of this is that sometimes Fermat got his stuff wrong, but usually it was correct. So did his proof really work *or* ... did he actually have a proof at all? Maybe he was just teasing everybody! (Our very own Professor Fiendish would have loved Pierre de Fermat and his Fiendish Feorem.) Whichever it was, it worked! Mathsie types were weeping and screaming over this for over 350 years until...

In 1993 a maths genius called Andrew Wiles finally came up with a proof. It had taken him seven years of solid brain power, and used some of the most murderous maths ever invented, including a ton of stuff that Fermat would never have heard of.

It involved long lectures, masses of analysis and cages full of experts going goggle-eyed trying to understand how he'd done it. Now obviously you'd like to know exactly how his proof works so here's the basic plan for the first bit.

You kick off with a study of modular elliptic curves and look at some Galois representations starting with a few refinements to Mazur's deformation theory which obviously leads on to Hecke rings. Off we go then...

Let p be an odd prime. Let Σ be a finite set of primes including p and let Q_Σ be the maximum extension of Q unramified outside this set and ∞. Fix an embedding of $\bar{Q}$ and so also of Q_Σ in C. D_q is your decomposition group for all primes q in Z. Suppose that k is a finite field of characteristic p and that p_0: $\text{Gal}(Q_\Sigma/Q) \to GL_2(k)$ is an irreducible representation.

Once you've got this set up, you wiggle it about a bit and end up with some results which you can use to interpret generalized cotangent spaces as Selmer groups which you can then relate to the Bloch-Kato conjecture if you want a bit of a laugh (but this last bit isn't vital).

By now any self-respecting Murderous Maths reader will have no trouble working out how the next few hundred pages go, but the sad news is that you're too late. Andrew Wiles got there first and so in the whole history of maths, his name is up there with the big guys and we are indeed blessed to be living on the same planet in his lifetime. Yes we are, don't sneer.

BUT … there's just one *teeny* doubt! If Fermat did have a proof was it just half a page of scribbles with "There, I told you so!" written at the end?

By the way, just to give you the vaguest sniff of what's involved with this sort of problem, the genius Euler had said that there were no possible answers to this beauty (which you'll notice has an extra set of brackets): $(\ )^4 + (\ )^4 + (\ )^4 = (\ )^4$

Nobody could quite prove he was right, but after 200 years everyone had become pretty dead certain there were no numbers that would fit in the gaps and work.

But then in 1988 somebody called Naom Elkies came up with…

$$2{,}682{,}440^4 + 15{,}365{,}639^4 + 18{,}796{,}760^4 = 20{,}615{,}673^4$$
... which is obvious when you look at it, isn't it?

In fact it's nearly as obvious as this one that was found a bit later:

$$95{,}800^4 + 217{,}519^4 + 414{,}560^4 = 422{,}481^4$$

FORTUNES AND PHOBIAS

Did you know that you can tell your fortune using numbers?

AHA! 2475.62 MEANS I'M ABOUT TO GO ON A SHORT, DARK JOURNEY!

Over 10,000 years ago the ancient Egyptians and Babylonians thought numbers were so marvellous that they got a bit bored of just using them for sums so they invented ways of telling fortunes with them. This has given us all a bit of fun ever since and in particular the ancient Greek Pythagoras took it all very seriously – but then he and his disciples worshipped numbers so they would, wouldn't they?

These days fortune-telling from numbers has all been boiled down to a few rather slick procedures called *numerology*. It's fair to say that most fortune-tellers take themselves rather seriously and stare at you without blinking for ages, but numerologists tend to be rather jolly and don't mind if you don't believe them. That's just as well because needless to say it's fair old rubbish, but that's never stopped anything from getting itself into a Murderous Maths book. Besides, it's a good way of practising a few quick sums.

How to tell your fortune with numbers

You take a bit of information about yourself and convert it into one of the key numbers, which are 1

71

to 9 or 11 or 22. You then check the result on this chart (which we've kept as simple as possible). By the way, if you get an 11 or 22, you don't add 1 + 1 or 2 + 2 because these are "master numbers" which make you *very special*. Oooh!

KEY NUMBER	YOU ARE...
1	BOSSY, IMPULSIVE AND FULL OF YOURSELF.
2	AFFECTIONATE, SHY, DEEP THINKER.
3	PARTY ANIMAL, ENTHUSIASTIC AND PROBABLY RATHER IRRITATING.
4	RELIABLE WORKER AND GOOD ORGANIZER.
5	ADVENTUROUS AND RESTLESS, TRY ANYTHING ONCE.
6	DOMESTICATED AND SENSIBLE, WITH STRONG OPINIONS.
7	A LONER WHOSE MIND IS AWAY WITH THE FAIRIES...
8	MONEY DRIVEN AND RUTHLESS.
9	AMAZING IMAGINATION, RARELY LOOKS SMART.
11	ARTISTIC, IMPRACTICAL, BUT INSPIRING TO TALK TO.
22	DETERMINED, PRACTICAL AND ON A MISSION TO IMPROVE THE WORLD.

There are loads of different key numbers you can generate to find out different things but we'll only deal with a few of them here.

Your birthpath number
This number tells you what you're supposed to be like:
- Write out your birthday in numbers – so if you were born on 19th January 1931 you'd put 19/01/31.
- Add up the digits – so here we get $1 + 9 + 0 + 1 + 3 + 1 = 15$.

- Keep going until you get 1, 2, 3, 4, 5, 6, 7, 8, 9, 11 or 22. Here we get $1+5=6$.
- Check the chart. If your birthpath is 6 then you're a sensible and domesticated person who knows their own mind, which is nice.

It will come as no surprise to you to learn that our noble author's birthpath produces the number 22 which goes to show that sometimes numerology is marvellously accurate.

What rubbish! Writing naff books isn't going to improve anything!

Huh. The artist was supposed to draw a stunning portrait of our noble author in that gap but obviously Mr Reeve got jealous because his birthpath number is BORING. (Which again shows how accurate it is.)

Your destiny number
This number is supposed to indicate what you'll end up doing.
- Write out your full name, e.g. Pongo McWhiffy.
- Convert each letter into a digit using this chart:

1	2	3	4	5	6	7	8	9
A	B	C	D	E	F	G	H	I
J	K	L	M	N	O	P	Q	R
S	T	U	V	W	X	Y	Z	

So Pongo McWhiffy becomes 76576 43589667.

- Add the digits to convert them into a key number. In Pongo's case his full name adds up to 79: then $7+9=16$, then $1+6=7$.
- Look at the chart ... and it tells us that Pongo has become a loner whose mind is away with the fairies. Let's see if this is right:

Your heart and personality numbers...

If you just use the vowels in your name to make a key number you find your inner **heart** (in other words what you're really like deep down inside). On the other hand if you just use the consonants in your name, you find what your outer **personality** is like. If you get exactly the same number for both, then you are well balanced!

Test the system yourself

First have a look at the key number chart and decide what sort of person you think you are. THEN work out your birthpath number and see if it agrees with you. We tried destiny, heart and personality numbers out on some Murderous Maths characters. See if you can match our results!

BLADE BOCCELLI　　VERONICA GUMFLOSS　　GRIZELDA　　EVIL GOLLARK

1 Which deep down party animal has ended up bossy and impulsive?

2 Who has turned out to be a loner – away with the fairies?

3 Who is domesticated and sensible deep down inside? (This'll surprise you!)

4 And who (deep down inside) is ruthless about money, outwardly seems to be adventurous but has really turned out to be a good solid worker?

Answers: 1 Veronica **2** Gollark **3** Grizelda **4** Blade

Make up your own meanings!

There are loads of other official meanings to the numbers – such as if your birthday falls on the 12th of the month you should have a winning personality. How did they work that out? Who knows, but there's no reason why you shouldn't have a go. Think about the people whose birthdays you know and then choose appropriate numbers to fill in the boxes yourself*:

If your birthday is on the ☐ of the month then you are a talented charming generous witty superstar.

If your birthday is on the ☐ of the month then you are a lazy, self-centred slob.

If your birthday is on the ☐ of the month then you have never ever changed your underwear.

If your birthday is on the ☐ of the month then you are an utter and total creep.

*Note from the Murderous Maths legal team: we take no responsibility for any numbers written in the above boxes.

In fact, there's no reason why you shouldn't make up your own "key number" chart with a few more interesting characteristics on it (such as "6 = you like drinking tea from an old slipper" or "11 = you think you're so flippin' gorgeous"). You can then try it out on your friends' names and birthdays and have a good laugh.

Lucky numbers

Almost everybody thinks they have a particular lucky number – often it's the day of the month they were born on. Otherwise numbers like 3 or 7 are quite popular – but did you know that there's a maths formula for producing lucky numbers? It was invented by Stanislaw Ulam in 1955 and here's what to do:

Write out as many numbers as you can be bothered with:

1 2 3 4 5 6 7 8 9 10 11 12 13 14 15 16 17 18 19 20
21 22 23 24 25 26 27 28 29 30 31 32 33 34 35
36 37 38 39 40 41 42 43 44 45 46 47 48 49 …

Ignore the 1 and see what the next number is, which is 2, so go along getting rid of every *second* number…

1   3   5   7   9   11   13   15   17   19
21   23   25   27   29   31   33   35
37   39   41   43   45   47   49 …

Check the next number left in the list which is now 3. Go along and get rid of every *third* number…

1   3   7   9   13   15   19
21   25   27   31   33
37   39   43   45   49 …

Check the next number which is now 7. Go along and get rid of every *seventh* number…

1   3   7   9   13   15
21   25   27   31   33
37   43   45   49 …

Check the next number which is now 9. Go along and get rid of every *ninth* number…

1   3   7   9   13   15
21   25   31   33
37   43   45   49 …

…and so on.

What you are left with is the list of **lucky numbers**. Why are they called lucky? Because you've killed off all the others and these are the survivors.

Like any other pattern of numbers, the Pure Mathematicians stare at them until their eyes pop, hoping to notice something brilliant about them. The best they can do here is decide that lucky numbers are a bit like prime numbers because there's about the same amount of them. Also they *think* Goldbach's Conjecture (on page 107) works, i.e. you can make any even number by adding two lucky numbers. However, lucky numbers do have at least one feeble use – superstitious Pure Mathematicians often use them on their lottery tickets.

You might be surprised that the list of lucky numbers includes the number 13 because a lot of people think it's unlucky. In fact some people have... **triskaidekaphobia** (fear of the number 13).

You can even have paraskavedekatriaphobia which is fear of Friday the 13th. So what are phobias all about?

Some people are scared of being stuck in small places such as a lift and that's known as

AN ARACHNOPHOBIC PERSON STUCK IN A COAL CELLAR WITH A NYCTOPHOBIC SPIDER.

EEK!

GIBBER!

claustrophobia. If you're scared of the dark, then you're a nyctophobic. Quite a lot of people are scared of spiders which is called arachnophobia and nearly everybody has a bit of ophidiophobia which is snakes. And if you're scared of being stuck in a dark lift with a load of spiders and snakes that's called being sensible.

There are loads of different phobias and although you might have a good snigger at an eisoptrophobic[1] putting on make-up, a genuphobic[2] watching a football match or a dishabiliophobic's[3] trousers falling down, it isn't much fun for the victim.

([1]mirrors; [2]knees; [3]undressing in public.)

A hippopotomonstrosesquippedaliophobic wouldn't like "hippopotomonstrosesquippedaliophobic" because it's a fear of long words. And if you've got scatophobia you won't be enjoying this book much because (putting it politely) that's a fear of rubbish. But out of all the billions of different numbers, why does the number 13 have its own phobia? Nobody knows for sure, but here are three of the theories so you can choose your own:

- 13 is unlucky because it's one more than 12. Suppose you've got a bag of 12 liver sandwiches and you have to share them between Urgum the Axeman and Grizelda the Grisly. No worries, they get 6 each. But what if Hunja the Headless turns up? You can still divide the sandwiches fairly by giving them 4 each and everybody will be happy with you.  Even if Mungoid the Jungoid toddles up, you can give them all three each and there's no problems. It was lucky you had 12 sandwiches to start with, wasn't it? But it wouldn't have been so lucky if you'd had 13.

- 13 is unlucky because in the ancient Hebrew alphabet, the 13th letter was "M" and that's the first letter of the word "mavet" which means death.

- 13 is unlucky because at the Last Supper in which Jesus Christ was betrayed he was sitting there with his 12 disciples – making 13 people sitting round the table.

All sorts of people avoid the number 13 – a lot of hotels do not have a room number 13, and some really big hotels don't even have a floor numbered 13.

Posh people consider it very bad luck to have 13 people at a dinner table. Here's some of the things they do to avoid it:

Although there's a good reason for a lot of phobias (nobody would blame you for having atomosophobia which is fear of atomic explosions) the lovely thing about triskaidekaphobia is that it's just daft. What's even better is that over the centuries it's affected all sorts of people including the French Emperor Napoleon and Henry Ford who started the massive Ford motor company. So what happens if you meet some serious triskaidekaphobics and tell them that they are being silly? If they know their stuff they'll come back with their big trump card:

WHAT ABOUT APOLLO 13?

The 17 Apollo rockets were sent up one at a time to investigate the moon and most famously the first man on the moon, stepped out of Apollo 11. However, *nearly* as famously, Apollo *13* exploded up in space on *13*th April 1970.

THERE'S MORE TO IT THAN THAT!

THE DATE OF THE ROCKET LAUNCH WAS 11TH APRIL 1970. IF YOU WRITE THIS DATE OUT AS 11/4/70 THEN ADD UP THE DIGITS, YOU GET 1+1+4+7+0=13!

AND... THE LAUNCH-TIME WAS AROUND LUNCH TIME. 13:13 TO BE PRECISE!

Maybe Apollo 13 was unlucky, but amazingly enough the astronauts *did* manage to get back to earth safely in their tiny lunar landing module. It would have been a bit like crossing the Atlantic Ocean in a barrel – but they made it. So maybe 13 was extremely lucky after all? AND ... everybody seems to forget that Apollo 1 caught fire on the launch pad, killing all three astronauts. So why isn't 1 an unlucky number then?

Of course, one reason that 13 is thought to be unlucky is that people like to *make* it unlucky...

City: Chicago, Illinois, U.S.A.
Place: Luigi's Diner, Upper Main Street
Date: 5 October 1929
Time: 10.25 p.m.

"Hey Luigi, bring the bill," said Ma Butcher. "That was one great dinner."

"Thank you, ma'am," said Luigi.

"And what a nice quiet place you have here. Myself and Long Jake like it quiet."

Luigi liked it quiet too, especially as he thought back to how the evening had started. The four Gabrianni brothers had arrived just as the three Boccellis had seated themselves around the large central table.

"Hoi, move it you finks," Half-smile Gabrianni had said. "This is the biggest table in the joint and we is four of us and you is just three of you."

"Yeah," said the Weasel. "So you go get yourselves tucked away into that nice small booth by the sink out of sight."

"Maybe we don't fit into a nice small booth," drawled Blade Boccelli.

"Then allow me to assist you," said Chainsaw Charlie, opening his chainsaw-shaped suitcase and pulling out a chainsaw-shaped chainsaw.

"You don't scare us with that butter knife," scoffed Blade.

The Weasel pulled his gun from his belt.

"Or that peashooter," sniggered One-Finger Jimmy.

Half-smile pulled his bull whip from under his hat.

"I've eaten liquorice strings bigger than that," sneered Porky.

Numbers pulled his finger from his nose. "OK, who wants some of this?" he said.

"Go easy, friend!" muttered Blade, getting up from the table.

"This is a respectable place!" pleaded Jimmy, backing away.

"Yeah," said Porky. "People gotta eat here. Keep it clean."

Down behind the counter, Luigi had been bracing himself for the big fight, but suddenly a miracle had happened. From the doorway, a long thin knife whistled through the air and thudded into the exact centre of the table. Even before it had stopped quivering, a hat gently flew over and landed neatly on the handle.

"Argh!" screamed the seven men in harmony, accidentally producing a musical chord of E flat minor 7.

"Now where did I hang my hat?" came a slow voice. "'Cos wherever I hang my hat is where I eat."

"Oh mamma mia!" whimpered Luigi as he peered over the counter. A long grey man was ushering a short jewelled woman towards the centre table.

"Well if it isn't Blade and his little friends!" exclaimed Ma Butcher. "Playing at cowboys too, how cute. But this is a restaurant, so why don't you all just run along and play outside."

"Pardon us, ma'am," Weasel blushed nervously. "But we were just about to have dinner."

"You eat with a gun in your hand?" said Ma Butcher. "Well mercy me. I was taught that grown-ups used a fork. You tell them why Long Jake."

"That way you don't blow your teeth through the back of your head."

Long Jake slowly drew his hand from his pocket and the seven men stepped backwards across the room in perfect unison. It was such a neat move that

Luigi almost clapped. But instead of a gun, Jake only produced a handkerchief and flicked a few errant crumbs from two of the chairs. Ma Butcher was about to sit when she looked across at the men in surprise.

"Still here, boys?"

"No!" they all replied.

"Well you sure look like you're here, which is a shame because Jake and I would appreciate a little privacy."

"There's a nice small booth with a curtain," said Blade.

"Right over in the corner by the sink," added Numbers. "It's real cosy."

"Now that's very obliging of you all," said Ma Butcher. "Isn't it, Jake?"

The long man smiled. It was the sort of smile you'd expect on someone who had just enjoyed eating a raw puppy.

Moments later when Benni the waiter came out of the kitchen, it was all he could do not to explode with laughter. The booth had been designed for young couples who didn't mind having to sit very close. It was clearly not designed to have seven grown men crammed around, under and on top of the table.

"You gentlemen OK in there?" he asked.

"We're fine," gasped Chainsaw through clenched teeth. "Just fine."

"Shall I bring a menu?"

"Er ... we don't really have room. Just bring one bowl of spaghetti and one bottle of vino and some drinking straws. We'll work something out."

And thus the evening passed peacefully.

"Hey, Benni," whispered Blade an hour later. "Can we get the bill, please?"

"Coming right over, Mr Boccelli," said Benni the waiter, but as he crossed the room, Ma Butcher took the bill from him.

"Seventy cents?" she exclaimed. "Is that all? How pitiful that you've all had to share to save money. I'd no idea business was so bad."

"We're doin' just fine, ma'am," said Weasel. "And we got it worked out nice because there's seven of us, so we each pay er..."

"We each pay ten cents," said Numbers, holding out the money. "Ten by seven makes seventy."

Benni took the cash over to Luigi at the counter.

"Well, it was sure kind of you to let us have the big table," said Ma Butcher getting up to put on her coat. "So kind in fact, that we insist on paying for the vino. How much was the wine, Luigi?"

"Thirteen cents, ma'am."

"Ooh, the fancy stuff!" she remarked. "Well, let's hope that number thirteen's not going to be unlucky, eh boys?"

Long Jake grinned and dropped 13 cents into Luigi's hand.

"Thank you, ma'am," said Blade.

Luigi frowned at the money laid in front of him.

"Er, Benni, there's seven guys gave ten cents each, so that makes 70. But Jake paid 13 of it, so you better hand back 13 cents."

Each man held out his hand and Benni put a one cent coin into it.

"I got six cents left boss. How do I split it with seven guys?"

"How about we give Benni a tip?" said Porky. "After all, he's the one who has to clear up the booth and it is kind of messy."

They murmured agreement. Benni was less than impressed.

"Jees. Six whole cents," he muttered. "At last I can take my mother on that trip to Europe she always dreamed of."

"So everyone's happy!" chuckled Ma Butcher from the doorway. "That's good, but the funny thing is that you guys paid 70 cents to start with. But then all seven of you each got a cent back so that makes 63 cents. Benni has got 6 cents so that makes a total of 69 cents. It's just a thought but .... *who's got the missing cent?*"

The door closed and immediately the seven men turned on each other.

"Oh NO!" moaned Luigi, ducking behind the counter again.

Can you see where the extra cent went?

Answer: This is a version of a classic old riddle which has fooled all sorts of people for years. To get the answer you have to think what the gangsters' final bill came to. To start with the bill was 70 cents, but Ma Butcher paid 13 cents so the final bill was 70–13 = 57 cents. As they paid 70 cents and then got 7 cents back, in total they paid 63 cents. This includes 57 cents for the bill plus 6 cents for Benni. 63 cents = 57 cents + 6 cents.

PRIME SUSPECTS

The good news about this chapter is that we avoid fractions. Not interested, unwanted, don't care. Yippee. We're only interested in *whole numbers* or "integers". You have to adjust your thinking a bit, so first of all unscrew the side of your head and remove the "fractions" chip from your brain.

Now when a sum comes along such as $7 \div 2$ you just say "it can't be done!" Let's test it on some people.

Seven evil Gollarks from the planet Zog are cruising in two space capsules. They want to have the same number in both capsules but it *can't be done*.

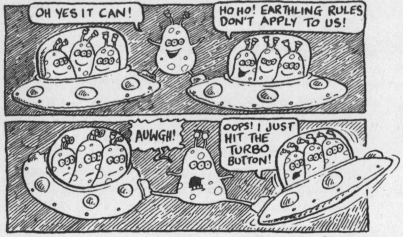

Let that be a lesson to you. When Murderous Maths lays down a few rules, they apply to *everyone*. Even evil Gollarks.

The only way the seven Gollarks could get exactly the same number in each capsule would have been to change the number of capsules. They would have had two choices: either one big capsule holding seven Gollarks, or seven little capsules each holding one Gollark. In terms of maths, this is because seven is a **prime** number and it obeys one of the most fundamental rules of the universe:

> **A prime number can only be divided exactly by itself and one.**

And that's why you can't split the number seven up in any other way.

But the good news for our Gollarks is that there are only six of them left which gives them a lot more choices. They could have one capsule with six Gollarks, six capsules with one Gollark, *or* three capsules with two Gollarks or two capsules with three Gollarks. This is because six will divide by 1, 2, 3 and 6. Any number that will divide by other numbers apart from itself and 1 is called a **composite** number. The numbers it will divide by are **factors** – so the factors of 6 are 1, 2, 3 and 6.

Mind you, even this doesn't help the Gollarks much:

The smallest prime numbers

2 is definitely a prime number because it only divides by 2 and 1. No problems there. 3 is also a prime number because it only divides by 3 and 1. However, 4 is *not* a prime number because as well as dividing by 4 and 1, it will also divide by 2. (In fact, 2 is the only even prime number, because *all* other even numbers will divide by 2.) You can go on checking each number in turn and find that the list of prime numbers starts 2, 3, 5, 7, 11, 13, 17,19, 23, 29 ... and so on.

Stand by for the big question though... *What about 1?*

This is one of our favourite questions in Murderous Maths because the number 1 gives us a rare and wonderful glimpse into the sort of thing that makes Pure Mathematicians bang their heads against walls.

It's very tempting to have a good snigger at Pure Mathematicians, but the Murderous Maths Organization decided to take the primeness or compositeness of 1 extremely seriously. At great expense we conducted an international survey of 100 million people and here are the results:

Is one a prime number?

Yes 7
No 8
Don't know 211
Don't care 99,999,774

So at last, conclusive proof that 1 is NOT prime by 8 votes to 7.

Primes v. composites – a one-sided fight

If you think all numbers are pretty much the same, you're in for a shock. If numbers were people then prime numbers would be sweaty wrestlers and composite numbers would be weedy ballroom dancers. True. Wanna know why? Because although the dancers can dazzle and delight us, when it comes down to the nitty gritty, the sweaty wrestlers can rip them to bits.

Let's meet one of each and see how they get on:

Oh dear. Composite numbers should really be more careful because a sweaty wrestling prime doesn't take too kindly to this sort of remark. He gets his prime mates round.

Breaking a number into its prime factors is rather a nasty process but if you're feeling tough enough to try it yourself you'll find the instructions in *The Mean and Vulgar Bits*. All we need to know for now is that *any* composite number can be made by multiplying two or more prime numbers together. In the case of 90 you'll find that $2 \times 3 \times 3 \times 5 = 90$. This means the **prime factors** of 90 are 2, 3, 3 and 5. (It's important to include both threes.)

To get the other factors of 90, just move all the prime factors (including both the 3s) around into different groups like this: $(2 \times 3) \times (3 \times 5) = 90$

If you work out the bits inside the brackets, you'll finish with $6 \times 15 = 90$. This tells us that two more factors of 90 are 6 and 15. How about these:

$2 \times (3 \times 3 \times 5) = 2 \times 45 = 90$ so 2 and 45 are factors

$(3 \times 3) \times (2 \times 5) = 9 \times 10 = 90$ so 9 and 10 are factors

$(2 \times 3 \times 3) \times 5 = 18 \times 5 = 90$ so 18 and 5 are also factors

$(2 \times 3 \times 5) \times 3 = 30 \times 3 = 90$ so 30 and 3 are even more factors.

And that's about it.

This trick doesn't just work on 90. If you break *any* composite number into its prime factors, you can find all the other factors that number has.

Tough and weedy numbers

There are a few basic rules about how primes and composites get on. If in doubt, remember to imagine them as tough wrestlers and weedy dancers.

THE BIG IMPORTANT RULE:

There are *always* two or more prime numbers that can divide their way into a composite number. E.g. 132 has prime factors 2, 2, 3 and

11. 169 only has two prime factors 13 and 13 which shows you that the prime factors don't have to be different. Primes are tough and can always pull composite numbers apart.

THE RULES THAT FOLLOW ON FROM THE BIG IMPORTANT RULE:

- Composite numbers can *never* divide their way into prime numbers. It's pathetic to watch them even try.
- If you've got a number that can't be divided by any prime number, it has to be an even bigger prime number itself (e.g. 521 can't be divided by any other prime number, so it must be prime).
- If prime numbers won't divide into a number, then composite numbers haven't a chance. Go on – get some composite numbers such as 4 or 15 or 28 and try to divide them into 521. You'll never do it because we've just seen 521 has to be prime.

AN UTTERLY FEEBLE RULE:

Sometimes composite numbers can divide into other composite numbers, but nobody cares much. $48 \div 8 = 6$ is all very cute and handy, but it's hardly at the cutting edge of maths.

How to check if a number is prime

You'll probably want to grab a calculator for this unless you're dealing with smallish numbers or you're feeling particularly brilliant. All you do is pick a mystery number and divide it by each of the prime numbers in turn starting with 2.

- If you get an exact answer at any point then the mystery number is *not* prime.
- Keep going until the answer is smaller than the prime number you just tried.

Let's try testing the number 883.

First divide by 2:

$883 \div 2 = 441.5$ Obviously 883 will not divide by 2 exactly because only even numbers divide by 2. (This result also tells us that 883 won't divide by multiples of 2 such as 4, 6, 8, 10 ... and so on.)

Now try the next prime number which is 3:

$883 \div 3 = 294.3333$ No good – remember we're looking for an exact answer.

Next we try 5...   Actually we won't bother trying 5 because 883 doesn't end in 0 or 5, so we know it won't work. (By the way, we know now that 883 won't divide by *any* multiple of 3 either, such as 3, 6, 9, 12, 15...)

Next you try dividing by 7, then 11, then 13, then 17, then 19 then 23 then 29 and you'll find that none of them divide exactly.

Eventually you get to 31 and reach this result:

$883 \div 31 = 28.48387$ This is EXCITING!

You'll see the answer is less than 31 which means that we don't need to go on. We've found that 883 is a prime number!

When you've understood this, it's time for a game of...

Prime suspects

Some villains have broken into Pongo McWhiffy's Burger Van and eaten his supply of pickled sprouts. The detective Sheerluck Holmes has rounded up the usual suspects, but how can he find which ones are guilty? He *could* make them all sit in a bath of water and watch out for green bubbles...

Sheerluck does have one clue – the pickled sprouts are slightly harder to chew than the tyres on Pongo's van so anybody eating one would need to be dead tough. It's no surprise that the sprout thieves all have tough prime ID numbers, so can you help Sheerluck find the thieves?

Answers: The thieves are 557, 941, and 929. The other numbers are composite: 779 = 19 × 41, 623 = 7 × 89, and 841 = 29 × 29.

If you want to check some really big numbers, there's a special prime number checker on *www.murderousmaths.co.uk*.

Prime patterns

Pure Mathematicians have spent thousands of years trying to predict a pattern of which numbers will be prime, but they haven't had much luck. At one point they thought that a row of threes followed by a one would be prime. They tried 31 331 3,331 33,331 and 333,331 and found they were all prime. Even 3,333,331 turned out prime and so did 33,333,331. They all got terribly excited until 333,333,331 turned out to be $19,607,843 \times 17$ so it was a weedy composite number after all.

About 400 years ago a French monk called Marin Mersenne lost a lot of sleep by trying different powers of 2 and then subtracting 1 to make prime numbers. A simple example is $(2^5 - 1)$ which is the quick way of writing $2 \times 2 \times 2 \times 2 \times 2 - 1$. This comes to $32 - 1 = 31$. Prime numbers that fit this formula are called Mersenne primes. Unfortunately, when it comes to nice reliable patterns this formula comes with three bits of bad news:

- If your power of 2 isn't a prime then the formula never works. For instance 6 is not prime and therefore $(2^6 - 1)$ isn't prime either. It makes 63 which is 7×9.
- Even if your power is prime, the formula still might not give you a prime. 11 is a nice rough tough prime number, but $(2^{11} - 1) = 2,047$ which is 23×89.
- There are trillions of prime numbers that don't fit the Mersenne formula.

Actually there's one bit of good news for Father Mersenne because there's a special use for his Mersenne primes in the Perfectly useless numbers chapter. But the bad news for him is that this use for Mersenne primes was thought of about 2,000 years before he was even alive.

A prime example of a Murderous Maths hero

While Father Mersenne was alive, he decided that $(2^{67} - 1)$ was a prime number, and nobody disagreed with him until one October day in New York, 1903…

It's a true story and all in the days before computers. Just imagine the brain effort it must have taken to find those two factors of $(2^{67} - 1)$ especially when nobody else thought that they even existed! As for our hero, Dr Cole only had four words to say on the matter. When he was asked "how long did it take you to find those factors?" he replied:

Three years of Sundays.

How many prime numbers are there altogether? Lots and lots and then some more.

If you want to understand why, then open the window. We're going to bring on a massive Murderous Maths star now and you're going to need some fresh air. Partly because this ancient Greek is over 2,000 years old but mainly to stop your brain overheating. Ready? Here we go then...

Euclid wrote the first ever murderous maths book, although it looked a bit different to the new groovy item that you're clutching today. It was 13 volumes long and called "Elements" and it seems the covers were painted by one Philippes Reevos. Elements was packed with top stuff including this beauty:

EVEN IF YOU THINK OF THE BIGGEST PRIME NUMBER YOU CAN, THERE WILL ALWAYS BE A BIGGER ONE.

Well that's not *exactly* how he said it, but you get the general idea. It works a bit like this:

- Think of the very biggest prime number you can. Let's be feeble and pretend that our biggest prime number is 13.

- Multiply it by every prime number underneath it right down to 2 – so you get $13 \times 11 \times 7 \times 5 \times 3 \times 2$ which comes to 30030.

- Add 1 to make 30031. Now we've just made a number that we know does not divide by 13, 11, 7, 5, 3 or 2 because whichever number you divide into it will have a remainder of 1. (And if it won't divide by any prime numbers, you automatically know that it won't divide by any weedy composite numbers either.)

- You now have two possibilities...

EITHER 30031 IS A PRIME NUMBER ITSELF... OR IF IT DIVIDES BY ANYTHING IT MUST DIVIDE BY BIGGER PRIME NUMBERS THAN 13.

- Either way, you've shown that there must be a bigger prime number than 13.

- Once you know there's a prime number bigger than 13, you start all over again with the bigger prime number and multiply it by all the smaller prime numbers then add 1 and then find there's an even *bigger* prime number and so on.

- Therefore there are an *unlimited* number of prime numbers. In other words: there are lots and lots and then some more.

As it turns out, 30031 is not a prime number, it is made from two prime factors multiplied together, and they both make 13 look rather weeny.

This leads to another problem that hits Pure Mathematicians such as Dr Cole right between the eyes. Even if they know that a massive number is not prime, trying to find exactly what numbers it divides by makes for some really murderous maths. For instance the number 11,111,111,111,111,111 isn't prime, but can you imagine being the person who found out that it comes from $2,071,723 \times 5,363,222,357$?

Just to get you into the swing, why not grab your calculator and see if you can find the two prime factors of 30031.

> **Answer:** $30031 = 59 \times 509$. Isn't it EASY when you know the answer?

What is the biggest prime number?
As we've just seen, there isn't a biggest one because they keep going up for ever. People concentrate a lot on finding bigger and bigger Mersenne primes – and on 14th November 2001 it was big cheers all round when they found that $(2^{13,466,917} - 1)$ was a prime number. The Murderous Maths printers did offer to type this number out in full for you, but as it has 4,053,946 digits this book would have needed more than 5,000 pages and would have cost you about £120.

Do prime numbers get rarer as they get bigger?
We think so because the bigger a number is, the more smaller numbers there are underneath it that might divide into it. However, we can't be sure

because it's hard to tell what happens when you reach galaxy-choking numbers that have billions and billions of digits. Anyway, here's a rough guide to numbers we *can* understand:

Between 1 and 20 there are 7 prime numbers: (2, 3, 7, 11, 13, 17, 19).

Between 101 and 120 there are 5 primes: (101, 103, 107, 109, 113).

Between 1,001 and 1,020 there are 3 primes: (1,009 1,013 1,019).

Between 10,001 and 10,020 there are 2 primes: (10,007 and 10,009).

Between 100,001 and 100,020 there are 2 primes: (100,003 and 100,019).

Between 1,000,001 and 1000,020 there is 1 prime... but can you find it?

Answer: 1,000,003 is prime. (If you thought 1,000,009 is prime, it comes from 293 × 3413.)

What's the saddest thing about prime numbers?
The sad thing arises because Pure Mathematicians *love* prime numbers, and you can't have a bit of love without a bit of sadness. Here's one of their favourite dreamboat prime numbers:

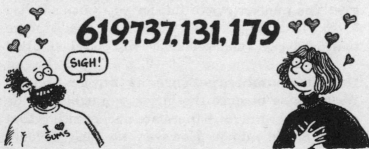

619,737,131,179

Why is it such a heart-throb? Because if you put a circle round any two digits next to each other, you get a little prime number. We'll invite our artist the Evil Reeve to demonstrate:

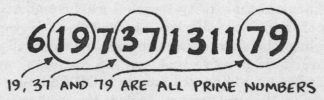

19, 37 AND 79 ARE ALL PRIME NUMBERS

What makes it so lovely is that all these little primes are different. 113 is the smallest prime number that does this (if you circle two digits you can get either 11 or 13), but 619,737,131,179 is the biggest.

Pure Mathematician's give different sorts of prime numbers different names, they write them out forwards, backwards and upside down, they play tricks with them, they teach them to sit, beg, roll over and let them sleep on the couch...

...BUT their little hearts are ever broken because they can't decide on the smallest one and they can't find the biggest one. And that's *so* sad.

You could win $1,000,000

Yes, you could – we're not kidding!

In 1742, a bloke called Christian Goldbach came up with the idea that you can make *any* even number by adding just two prime numbers together. e.g. $20 = 3 + 17$ or $36 = 7 + 29$.

This is called Goldbach's Conjecture – which means that everybody *thinks* it's true but nobody is absolutely sure one way or the other. The good bit is that it looks so simple but it's been driving some of the greatest maths brains mad for years. What makes it even worse for them is that there's usually somebody somewhere offering a big prize to anyone who can sort it out. The last time we checked, a book publisher* was offering $1,000,000 so if you're feeling a bit short of loose change this week, all you have to do is prove that you can make *any* even number by adding two primes – OR find an even number that you *can't* make from two primes.

*We'd like to add that the Murderous Maths publishers wouldn't offer 2p for something as useless as this. However, if you come up with something really good such as the everlasting chocolate bar or jet rocket boots or magic invisible potion, then we'll think about it.

The BBU section
Here are all the tests you need to know to see if a number divides by anything between 2 and 13. (BBU stands for Boring But Useful). Each test has one or more of these signs to let you know what you're in for.

 NO BRAIN REQUIRED.

 SO EASY – IT'S A PIECE OF CAKE!

 IF YOU CAN MAKE THIS WORK YOU'RE DEAD COOL.

 A BIT TEDIOUS.

2 ☠ Any even number (i.e. it ends in 0, 2, 4, 6, 8) divides by 2. Easy!

3 🪨 Add up the digits in the number. If you test 8,749,788 you get $8+7+4+9+7+8+8=51$. Do it again until you get a single digit; so $5+1=6$. (This is called the **digital root** of the number.) If the digital root divides by 3 then so does the number. In this case 6 does divide by 3 and therefore 8,749,788 will divide by 3 too.

4 🪨 Look at the last two digits. If the "tens" digit is even then the last digit must be 0, 4 or 8. (So 35,784 will divide by 4 because the 8 is even and the last digit is 4.) If the "tens" digit is odd then the last digit must be 2 or 6. (So 476 will divide by 4 but 9,734 will not.)

5 ☠ It's got to end in 0 or 5.

6 🪨🕸 It's got to be even AND divide by 3.

7 🐧🕸 Take the last digit off your number and multiply it by 2. Subtract it from the other digits. If the answer divides by 7 (or is 0) so does your number! So for 119 you multiply $9 \times 2 = 18$. Then subtract $11 - 18 = -7$. This divides by 7 (don't worry if a minus turns up), so 119 divides by 7.

8 Look at the last 3 digits. If the "hundreds" digit is even, then if the last two digits divide by 8, so will your big number. If the "hundreds" digit is odd, then the last two digits must divide by 4 but NOT 8. (So 3,540 will not divide by 8 but 3,544 will.)

9 Work out the digital root (as if you are checking for 3). If you end up with 9 then the whole number will divide by 9. So to check 846 you do $8+4+6=18$ and then $1+8=9$. So 846 will divide by 9.

10 💀 It has to end in 0.

11 Put alternate $+$ and $-$ signs in front of each digit. So for 64,559 you put $+6-4+5-4+8$ then work out what the whole sum comes to. If the answer is 0 or divides by 11, then so does your big number. In this case $6-4+5-4+8=11$ so 64,559 *does* divide by 11.

12 💀 If it divides by 3 AND 4 then it divides by 12.

13 Take off the last digit and multiply it by 9. Subtract it from the other digits. If the answer divides by 13, then so does the original number! Let's try 754. Take off the 4 and multiply by 9 so $4 \times 9 = 36$. Then work out $75 - 36 = 39$. 39 does divide by 13, therefore so does 754!

And just as a special bonus....

19 You can test if a number divides by 19! Take off the last two digits, multiply them by 4 then add the answer to the other digits. If the answer divides by 19, then so does the original. Try 6,935. $35 \times 4 = 140$. Then add $69 + 140 = 209$. Do it again! $09 \times 4 = 36$ then $36 + 2 = 38$, which does divide by 19. So 6,935 divides by 19 too!

A day in the life of a Pure Mathematician

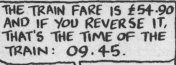

THE TRAIN FARE IS £54.90 AND IF YOU REVERSE IT, THAT'S THE TIME OF THE TRAIN: 09.45.

BUT DAD...

THE TRAIN GETS IN AT 11.56 AND THE SQUARE ROOT OF 1156 IS 34 — THE NUMBER OF PEOPLE AT THE CONFERENCE.

BUT DAD!

PAT PAT

STOP WORRYING, SUMSIE! EVERYTHING'S UNDER CONTROL!

SIGH...

BYE!

THE CURIOSITY SHOP

"Ting-a-ling" went the little bell as you entered.

"Welcome to my little emporium," said the odd-looking man with the false plastic nose behind the counter.

"Why have you got a false plastic nose?" you asked suspiciously.

"To hold on my false plastic beard, of course!"

Of course when you look back, you should have realized at once that something wasn't quite right. But your eye had been caught by the most amazing range of puzzles and teasers that you could ever have imagined. Here's what you found:

Last One Left

Pick any two-digit number. Multiply the digits together, then do it again and again until you only have one digit left (e.g. 34 gives $3 \times 4 = 12$ then $1 \times 2 = 2$).

Which two-digit number takes the longest to get down to one digit?

FREAKY FRACTIONS

If you want to cancel fractions usually you have to divide the top and the bottom by the same number. So if you have $\frac{12}{24}$ you divide both numbers by 12 to get $\frac{1}{2}$. What you *can't* do is just cross a "2" off the top and the bottom like this:

$$\frac{1\cancel{2}}{\cancel{2}4} = \frac{1}{4} \longleftarrow \text{YOU CAN'T DO THIS}$$

But there are one or two special cases where you can cross the same digit off the top and bottom! Check these...

$$\frac{16}{64} = \frac{1\cancel{6}}{\cancel{6}4} = \frac{1}{4} \qquad \frac{19}{95} = \frac{1\cancel{9}}{\cancel{9}5} = \frac{1}{5}$$

$$\frac{49}{98} = \frac{4\cancel{9}}{\cancel{9}8} = \frac{4}{8} = \frac{1}{2}$$

Can you find another fraction (both numbers less than 100) that works like this?

114

MR KAPREKAR'S AMAZING EXPERIMENTS

This is brilliant! Choose any four-digit number (so long as the digits are not all the same) then do this:

- Move the digits round to make the highest possible number.
- Move the digits round to make the lowest possible number.
- Subtract the lowest from the highest.
- Do the same thing again with your answer.
- Eventually you will be stuck with **6174**.

CHOOSE ANY FOUR-DIGIT
NUMBER SUCH AS... **9189**

REARRANGE DIGITS INTO
HIGHEST NUMBER ⟶ **9981**
AND LOWEST NUMBER ⟶ **1899**
THEN SUBTRACT TO GET ⟶ **8082**

REARRANGE TO HIGHEST **8820**
AND LOWEST AGAIN **0288**
SUBTRACT ⟶ **8532**

KEEP GOING UNTIL **8532**
YOU GET 6174 ⟶ **−2358**
= **6174**

AND IF YOU DO IT
ONCE MORE... **7641**
−1467
= **6174**

If you do the same process but start with a three-digit number, what number do you always get stuck with?

Final Digit Patterns

If you multiply 8×8 you get 64. Take the final digit and multiply it by 8 again: $4 \times 8 = 32$. Take the final digit and multiply it by 8: $2 \times 8 = 16$. Take the final digit and multiply it by 8: $6 \times 8 = 48$. The final digit has come back to 8! If you keep going the pattern would be 8-4-2-6-8-4-2-6-8-4-2-6-8...

If you try this with 2 you get $2 \times 2 = 4$ then $4 \times 2 = 8$ then $8 \times 2 = 16$ then $6 \times 2 = 12$ and so on, making the pattern 2-4-8-6-2-4-8-6-2-4-8-6... which is the same as the "8" pattern backwards.

Now try this game with the other numbers between 1 and 9. Can you find another pair that produce the same pattern but in reverse?

The Persistant Number

PUF Brain Drain

526,315,789,473,684,210 multiplied by any number between 2 and 18 uses all the same digits in the same order – the answer just starts in a different place! (There's also an extra 0 at the end.) Try it yourself – what do you get if you multiply it by 7?

Incidentally $1 \div 19 = 0 \cdot 0526315789473684210...$

"So have you enjoyed yourself?" says the man with the big plastic nose. He is clutching a book labelled: Solutions.

"Yes, thank you, but there are one or two answers I'd like to check in your book please!"

"Har har!" comes a diabolical laugh. Off comes the nose and the false beard and there he is... Professor Fiendish your arch-enemy. "I see my cunning disguise fooled you!"

Oh boy. How could you have been so stupid? Still, it's a good time to be cool, so you pretend not to recognize him.

"I'm sorry?" you say politely. "Have we met?"

"Surely you recognize me from your worst mathematical nightmares!" he cackles.

"Hmmm ... maybe if you took off those silly rubber ears," you suggest.

"I'm not wearing any rubber ears!" he snarls.

"Oh!" you say in surprise. "It must be those goofy yellow teeth then."

"Those are my *real* teeth!" he splutters.

"Well I give in. I suppose that badly fitted wig isn't helping, not to mention the silly glasses and as for the *smell*..."

"That does it!" he screams, ripping open a box and pulling out a set of chains. "You can be the first to try my own personal invention!"

"You'll never see inside the book unless you can break a link on my number chain."

How utterly diabolical! You are destined never to sleep again unless you can put your mind at rest with the answers.

Instructions to break the Chain:

Pick one of the numbered links.
If the number is EVEN halve it.
If the number is ODD subtract 1.
Keep going until you get to 0 and so make the link disappear.
You may NOT do more than 10 operations to break a link.

Can YOU find the only link which will break? The other answers are on that page of this book.

MAGIC FINGERS

Suppose you're counting from 1 to 10 or doing sums such as $7-3$. Which of these do you think is the most babyish:

- counting on your fingers
- sucking both your feet at once
- getting the answer wrong
- using a calculator?

As sad as counting on your fingers might look, it's much the best option. And if you have to use a calculator, well what can we say? It's about time you grew up, so get those shoes off and start sucking.

Multiplying up to 10
With a bit of mathsy magic, you can also use your fingers for multiplying! You just need to know your times tables from $1 \times 1 = 1$ up to $5 \times 5 = 25$, then you can go on to multiply any numbers between 6 and 10. Imagine your fingers are marked like this:

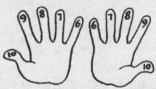

There are two separate jobs to do. You need to work out the "tens" and the extra "units". Let's try multiplying 7×8 to see how this works.

- Touch together the numbers 7 and 8 on your fingers.
- Imagine a worm sitting along your touching fingers.
- All the fingers underneath the worm count as 10 each, so just add them all up. (In this case it's $20 + 30 = 50$.)

- To get the extra units: multiply the fingers above the worm. (Here we've got three fingers on one side and two on the other: $3 \times 2 = 6$.)
- Add the tens and extra units together to get the answer. Here we have $50 + 6 = 56$ which is the correct answer because $7 \times 8 = 56$.

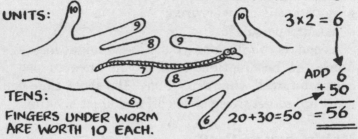

MULTIPLY FINGERS OVER WORM TO GET UNITS:

UNITS:

$3 \times 2 = 6$

ADD 6
$+ 50$

TENS:

FINGERS UNDER WORM ARE WORTH 10 EACH.

$20 + 30 = 50$ $= 56$

Be honest – it's good, isn't it? Here's how 6×7 would work out:

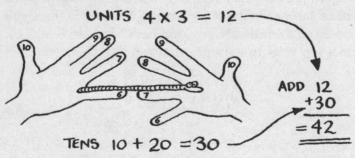

UNITS $4 \times 3 = 12$

ADD 12
$+ 30$
$= 42$

TENS $10 + 20 = 30$

Multiplying up to 15

The amazing thing is that you can use your fingers in a slightly different way to multiply any two numbers between 11 and 15. Suppose you want to multiply 12×14, you imagine that your fingers are numbered 11 to 15 and touch together the 12 and 14 fingers. Then do these quick sums:

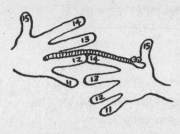

TENS: ADD UP FINGERS
UNDER WORM: 20+40=60
EXTRA UNITS: MULTIPLY FINGERS
UNDER WORM:
2×4=8
ADD AN EXTRA 100
TOTAL = 168
(AND YES – 12×14=168!)

Try doing some other sums such as 13×13 or 15×11. Just remember that for the extra units you use the fingers *under* the worm and don't forget to add on the extra 100.

Multiplying up to 20

You can even do sums like 17×19! Imagine your fingers are numbered 16 to 20 then touch together 17 and 19 and do this:

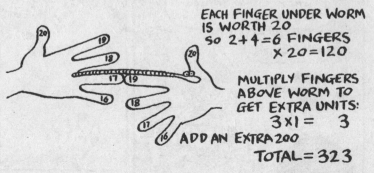

EACH FINGER UNDER WORM
IS WORTH 20
So 2+4=6 FINGERS
×20=120

MULTIPLY FINGERS
ABOVE WORM TO
GET EXTRA UNITS:
3×1 = 3
ADD AN EXTRA 200
TOTAL = 323

This time the fingers under the worm are each worth 20, and for the extra units you use the fingers *above* the worm. Finally, it's 200 that you need to add on to get the right answer.

121

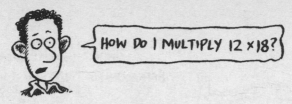

Life gets rather complicated if you're mixing numbers from different ranges unless you're prepared to have a bit of drastic surgery...

When fingers talk

LATE AT THE LAST CHANCE SALOON...

I BET I'M HOLDING A HIGHER CARD THAN YOU, BRETT.

OH YEAH?

BRETT WILL NEVER SUSPECT THAT I'VE ONLY GOT A THREE!

SHOVE

As Brett Shuffler and Riverboat Lil know, it's very easy to indicate any number between 1 and 10 with your fingers. But what about bigger numbers?

Let's be honest here. Standing on one leg with your toes showing can't be the most dignified way of indicating the number 15. Life would have been much easier for the spying bartender if he had a friend to help him cope with two of Lil's special cards...

1 LOT OF TEN + 5 UNITS
$1 \times 10 + 5 = 15$

5 LOTS OF TEN + 9 UNITS
$5 \times 10 + 9 = 59$

The bartender indicates the number of units, and the waitress indicates how many tens there are. It's a simple system, but the question is will Lil let them go on making signs behind her back?

Oh dear. How would the bartender indicate the number nine now? Before he could have stuck up nine fingers, but now that some of his fingers are bandaged together, the biggest number he can indicate is 8. The answer is that the waitress uses her fingers to indicate how many *eights* are in the number. This is how they would have to indicate Lil's cards now:

1 LOT OF 8 + 7 UNITS   7 LOTS OF 8 + 3 UNITS

1 × 8 + 7 = 15   7 × 8 + 3 = 56 + 3 = 59

Base 8

Usually when we write numbers, we use "base 10". This means that for any number less than ten we have different signs which are 0, 1, 2, 3, 4, 5, 6, 7, 8, and 9. However, when we write ten, we don't have a special sign for it, so we put a "1" and a "0" together like this: 10. We've got used to the fact that if there are two digits together, the digit on the left is worth *ten* times more. With a longer number such as 365 we can quickly see what each digit is worth because each position is worth ten times more than the position after it.

BASE TEN			THIS NUMBER IS:

$$3 \quad 6 \quad 5$$

TENS OF TENS   TENS   UNITS

=10X10
=100'S

$$3 \times 100 = 300$$
$$+ 6 \times 10 = 60$$
$$+ 5 \times 1 = 5$$
$$\text{TOTAL} = 365_{10}$$

(If you want to indicate that you're using base 10, you should put a little "10" afterwards like this: 365_{10}. This saves confusion as you'll see in a minute.)

We take for granted that numbers are in base 10 because we have 10 fingers, but when the bartender and waitress each lost the use of a couple of fingers, they had to use **base 8**.

Base 8 only has eight different signs: 0, 1, 2, 3, 4, 5, 6 and 7. When you want to write eight, you put a "1" and a "0" together to make 10 because now the digit on the left is worth *eight* times more.

Here's the tricky bit to understand: if you're using base 8 and you see "10" written down, it is NOT ten and you shouldn't call it ten. It's eight! What's more, if you see "365" in base eight, the "3" is in the "eights of eights" place so it is equal to 3×64. Here's how to see what 365_8 is worth in base 10:

BASE EIGHT	

$$3 \quad 6 \quad 5$$

EIGHTS OF EIGHTS = 8×8 = 64'S   EIGHTS   UNITS

THIS NUMBER IS:

$$3 \times 64 = 192$$
$$+ 6 \times 8 = 48$$
$$+ 5 \times 1 = \underline{\quad 5}$$
$$\text{TOTAL} = 245_{10}$$

There you are! $365_8 = 245_{10}$. It all looks a bit strange because "365" has a completely different meaning in base 8. For instance 365_8 is *not* the number of days in a year! When the waitress and barman were trying to indicate Lil's "59 of clubs", with 10 fingers each they could show 5 and 9. However, when they only had 8 fingers each they showed 7 and 3. That's because $73_8 = 59_{10}$.

When Halloween becomes Christmas

Sometimes base 8 is called the "octal" system and base 10 is called the "decimal" system. These words get shortened so that instead of writing $73_8 = 59_{10}$ you could put: oct 73 = dec 59. Here's something cute:

oct 31 = dec 25

Go on – test it and see!

CHRISTMAS ALREADY? BUT... HOW?

Other bases

The "10" system was started about 1,500 years ago by the Hindus and it was gradually improved, especially by the Arab traders. These are the signs they used for the digits:

HINDU $\quad$ 1 2 3 8 4 (7 (9 0

ARABIC $\quad$ 1 2 7 4 5 6 7 8 9 0

The ten system is the obvious one to use because we have ten fingers and thumbs (which you can also call digits), but other systems have also been in use such as the "20" system which was based on people's fingers *and toes*. Each digit is worth 20 times more than the digit on the right so the number 80 in base 10 would become 40 in base 20. This system is still remembered in France because their way of saying "eighty" is "quatre-vingts" which means "four twenties".

However, if you want to see a *really* cool system, you've got to go back almost 4,000 years to see the Babylonians using base 60. They had a way of writing numbers up to 59 using little arrowheads, but then to write sixty they would put their version of "10". Here's how Babylonians would write the number 15,834:

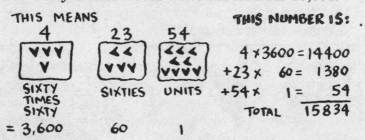

THIS MEANS

4	23	54
SIXTY TIMES SIXTY	SIXTIES	UNITS
= 3,600	60	1

THIS NUMBER IS:

$$4 \times 3600 = 14400$$
$$+23 \times \quad 60 = \quad 1380$$
$$+54 \times \quad 1 = \quad\quad 54$$
$$\text{TOTAL} \quad 15834$$

So why would anybody want to use base 60?

IT MAKES SUMS EASY!

OUR CALENDARS HAVE EXACTLY 360 DAYS IN THE YEAR — WHICH IS 6×60.

THERE ARE 360° IN A CIRCLE- USEFUL WHEN WE'RE MAPPING OUT THE SKY.

60 DIVIDES BY 2, 3, 4, 5, 6, 10, 12, 15, 20 AND 30.

They managed to do the most murderous sums in base 60 using numbers up to 17 digits long. In our modern base 10 these numbers would be up to 30,000,000,000,000,000,000,000,000,000 and of course they didn't have calculators to help them! By the way, did you ever wonder why we have 60 seconds in a minute and 60 minutes in an hour? You guessed it – it's all thanks to the Babylonians.

Different people around the world have been known to use all sorts of number bases. Isolated tribes would develop their own systems such as the 5 system based on the fingers of one hand or even the 3 system based on the knuckles of each finger. Sadly, most of these tribes have now been absorbed into the big bully world where everybody expects you to wear jeans, drink from plastic bottles, gibber down mobile phones and use the 10 system. But that doesn't mean to say that the 10 system has taken over completely!

The biggest number crunchers in the world don't have fingers, toes or knuckles, instead they just have switches. That's why special number systems are vital in the workings of...

Computers

In the old days computers were about the size of a church and were full of big magnets and wires and red hot valves and things that went CLUNK rather importantly. They didn't have fancy screens with mouse pointers to move around, so the only way they could tell you anything was by switching a few light bulbs on and off.

If your computer only had one light bulb on the front it could only give you two possible answers. That meant you were a bit limited in what questions you could ask it.

The problem was that if you asked it what $1+1$ equals, it couldn't show you the answer "2" with just one light bulb. However, if your computer was the Calcatronic Deluxe with two bulbs, then it could do this:

Even more excitingly, it could work out $1+2$.

The computer is working to the 2 base or **binary** system where each digit is worth twice as much as the digit on the right. By lighting both bulbs the computer is showing that the answer contains one "2" and one "1" making a total of three. This system has good news and bad news. The good news is you can display *any* number by switching light bulbs on and off. The bad news is that you need a lot of light bulbs!

The Calcatronic Miracle had seven bulbs, and here's what each bulb was worth:

64 32 16 8 4 2 1

You'll notice that the number over each bulb is 2 times the next number along. You'll also notice that the bulbs numbered 64, 8, 4 and 1 are lit up, so the computer is indicating the number $64 + 8 + 4 + 1 = 77$.

Here's how the same computer would show some other numbers, and how the numbers would be written in "binary":

NUMBER	WHAT EACH BULB IS WORTH							BINARY
	64	32	16	8	4	2	1	
2						○		10
5					○		○	101
31			○	○	○	○	○	11111
32		○						1000 00
100	○	○			○			1100100
127	○	○	○	○	○	○	○	1111111

These days computers aren't nearly such fun, but they do work in a very similar way. They tend to use lots of four-digit binary numbers, so the smallest is 0000 which makes zero and the biggest is 1111 which is 15. However when people are programming

132

the things up, punching in loads of 1's and 0's is a very dull job, so the computer accepts what's called the **hexadecimal** system which is the posh word for base 16. The fun bit is that in hexadecimal "10" means 16 so how *do* you write ten, eleven, twelve, thirteen, fourteen or fifteen? The answer is that you use letters A, B, C, D, E and F to represent them. Here's how some numbers convert to base 16:

BASE 10:	1	2	3	4	5	6	7	8	9	10	11	12	13	14	15	16
BASE 16:	1	2	3	4	5	6	7	8	9	A	B	C	D	E	F	10

BASE 10:	17	20	31	32	33	100	200	255	256	4095
BASE 16:	11	14	1F	20	21	64	C8	FF	100	FFF

Strange sums
If you've got a scientific calculator you might find you can choose which number base you use. Doing sums in different bases gives you some headbending results!

"Dec" is the normal 10 system.

"Bin" is the 2 system.

"Oct" is the 8 system.

"Hex" is the 16 system.

(If you can get a go on a computer, look at the calculator in the programmes/accessories section. You can probably switch it into scientific mode and then choose to put it in any of these bases.)

You'll find that in "BIN" mode you can only enter 0 or 1. In "OCT" mode you can't put in 8 or 9, but in "HEX" mode you can put in any digit or letter A-F.

Here are a few odd experiments to try:

- Put in some big numbers then change the base.
  E.g. 1234 in DEC becomes 10011010010 in BIN,
  2322 in OCT and 4D2 in HEX.
- When are numbers 2989, 4011 and 57007 BAD,
  FAB and DEAF?
- Try multiplying 11×11 in BIN. Then try the
  same sum in the other bases. The answers might
  look the same but they are not!
- Try some of the basic sums from the times tables
  in OCT and HEX such as 6×7 or 5×5. The
  answers come as a bit of a shock!

Finger numbers

When the barman regains the use of all his ten
fingers, he could display any number from 0 to 1023
using the binary system. Here's what each finger is
worth:

So when Lil was holding the 947 of diamonds,
Brett knew immediately...

Final message

All the way through this chapter we've been saying that you've got 10 fingers. However, if you're the sort of person who is simply BURSTING to write and tell us that in fact we have eight fingers and two thumbs, please be aware that in the Murderous Maths Office we have an old Calcatronic Problem Eliminator which was originally owned by Urgum the Axeman. It doesn't actually do any sums, but it does have a quaint way of dealing with irritating letters.

PERFECTLY USELESS NUMBERS

One of the most satisfyingly useless bits of maths are the **perfect numbers**. Only one qualification is required to be perfect: you have to "equal the sum of your factors". This sounds tedious, but if we look at the lowest perfect number, which is 6, we can see that the only whole numbers that divide exactly into 6 (apart from 6 itself) are 1, 2 and 3. What makes it perfect is that if you add all these factors up you get $1+2+3=6$.

The next perfect number is 28 and so if we add up all the factors: $1+2+4+7+14=28$.

In ancient times all sorts of different religious people found reasons to agree with the mathematicians about these numbers being perfect:

Unfortunately, you have to go a long way to get to the next perfect number which is 496 and after that it's 8,128. It must have been a lot harder trying to fit these numbers into the big scheme of things:

What's more, there was a big mystery:

The quest for perfection

What makes perfect numbers so funny to normal people (i.e. those of us who are not Pure Mathematicians) is when we stop to think of the effort that went into working these numbers out. Let's suppose the number 8,128 had just been discovered to be perfect, and you and a bunch of Pure Mathematician friends decided to sit down and see who could be first to find the next perfect number.

It doesn't bear thinking about, does it? Of course looking at the first perfect numbers 6, 28, 496, 8128 it would be reasonable to assume that the next perfect number would be in the 50,000 area. Just to make sure you don't miss it, you would probably start checking numbers from 20,000 and keep going up. Every time you check a different number, you can't help thinking "this could be the one!" and it's so exciting that you completely lose the ability to sleep. The more numbers that you check, the more exciting it gets, and too late you realize that searching for the next perfect number is like looking for a needle in a haystack.

By the time you had got to checking the number 100,000 you might suspect you had missed the perfect number you were looking for, so you would then go back to 20,000 and check all the numbers going down. After several sleepless years of checking and double-checking you would realize that there aren't any perfect numbers between 8,128 and 100,000 so you have to go on up above 100,000. Your quest for the next perfect number is now like looking for a needle in a haystack the size of Australia. At this point you would be asking yourselves:

ARE WE ABSOLUTELY SURE THAT THERE ARE ANY MORE PERFECT NUMBERS?

Oh boy! Not only are you looking for a needle in a haystack the size of Australia, it turns out that there might not be a needle there after all. But, of course, spending your life looking for something that might not be there makes perfect sense to you because you are Pure Mathematicians! Yes, you're all nutters, but you are also extremely courageous and dedicated to the point of lunacy and that's why normal people are rather fond of you and bring you meals and make sure you get washed occasionally.

You have finally reached the number 1,000,000 and checked it. You divide it up into all its factors, you add them up and with a sigh you realize that just like the last 991,872 numbers you have checked, it is not perfect. Surely it is time to give up? The last perfect number was 8,128 so by now you must have moved out of the range of perfect numbers. You and your friends have proved that there are only four of them, so you decide to give up the quest. You wave goodbye to the gang, and allow yourself to go to bed. You lie down, but you can't relax...

You try to sleep. You have fitful dreams about beautiful sets of numbers neatly sliding into 1,000,001 producing fabulous arrays of factors that neatly line up and total that magical target 1,000,001. You leap out of bed, and after several hours of frantic calculation you realize that it was all a dream. 1,000,001 is not perfect. But what about 1,000,002? And so on it goes. Many years later...

At last you are satisfied that there are only four perfect numbers. You can do no more to prove it. Slowly your eyelids close, your breathing becomes steady, yet, just as you are about to drift away into welcome oblivion, there is a tap at the door. At first you don't hear, but then the voice of one of your old friends calls out...

And sure enough, eventually you do find the next perfect number. It's not in the tens of millions, or even the hundreds of millions, but when you get to the thousands of millions you finally hit it.

The sad part is that you can't tell anyone because by the time you found it you had been a ghost for several hundreds of years.

The truth

Actually this story is a bit of a lie because there are a few ways that help you find perfect numbers, but it is still rather a hit and miss process which needs a lot of checking and it takes ages. To give you an idea of how long it takes, it was around 500 BC that people realized that 6 was equal to the sum of its factors. However, the key to perfect numbers didn't arrive until 275 BC when the brilliant Greek called Euclid worked out a formula for making them which is this:

$$2^{n-1} \times (2^n - 1)$$

Any nervous Murderous Maths readers may wish to skip this next bit because we're going to take on powers, primes and perfects. It's the sort of thing you'd pay good money to see at a circus when you're bored of people juggling swords. If you're feeling weedy, you can rejoin us at "The sad bit" just over the page, but if you feel sharp enough, read on.

What you have to do is pick a number for "n" and put it in the formula – but the important thing is that the bit inside the brackets must be a prime number. This can only happen if n itself is a prime number. (Do you remember Mersenne primes from the Prime suspects chapter? Here's where they come in.) In other words we only need to try swapping n for the prime numbers 2, 3, 5, 7, 11, 13, 17, 19 and so on.

Suppose you pick n to be equal to 2. When you work out the bit in the brackets you get $2^2 - 1$. This comes to $4 - 1$ which is 3. HOORAY – we've got a prime number, so we can now swap n for 2 in the whole formula. We get:

$2^{2-1} \times (2^2 - 1)$ which becomes $2^1 \times (2^2 - 1)$ and then: $2 \times (3) = 6$.

We know 6 is a perfect number, so it works!

Now let's try making n = 3. The bit in the brackets is $(2^3 - 1)$ which is $(8 - 1) = 7$. That's prime too, so the formula will work, and this time it gives the next perfect number which is 28.

Let's try the next prime numbers:

- $(2^5 - 1) = 31$ is prime! So when we put n = 5 into the formula we get: $2^{5-1} \times (2^5 - 1) = 2^4 \times (2^5 - 1) = 16 \times 31 = 496$. It's the next perfect number. Yahoo!

- $(2^7 - 1) = 127$ is prime! Putting n = 7 into the formula gives us the perfect number 8128.

- $(2^{11} - 1) = 2047$, but as we saw ages ago, this isn't prime because $23 \times 89 = 2047$. Dry your eyes, shoulders back and on we go...

- $(2^{13} - 1) = 8191$ is prime. So bash n = 13 into the formula and you get $2^{13-1} \times (2^{13} - 1) = 2^{12} \times (2^{13} - 1) = 4096 \times 8191 = 33,550,336$.

There! We just reached that next big perfect number and even if you didn't quite follow what was going on, you have to admit it was a whole lot quicker than dividing and adding up billions of big numbers.

By the way, the next values for "n" that give Mersenne primes and perfect numbers are 17, 19, 31 and then there's a MASSIVE leap to n = 61. We don't know why it's such a massive leap, but it just is.

143

The sad bit

Although Euclid invented his formula nearly 2,300 years ago, nobody actually managed to calculate the fifth perfect number until the year 1456 (which was more than *seventeen centuries* later). Even these days with fabulous great big computers steaming away around the clock, they could only work out the 39th perfect number when they found the 39th Mersenne prime in November 2001. To give  you an idea of what they are up against here's the 31st perfect number: $2^{216090} \times (2^{216091} - 1)$

As you can see, people normally keep these big perfect numbers written out with Euclid's formula. You're probably thinking what a lazy lot they are in the Murderous Maths factory, why don't they just work out the sum and print out the whole number properly? To be fair there's a very good reason for this – the 31st perfect number has 130,099 digits and so to print it would fill a complete book the same size as this one! It also goes without saying – it would be screamingly boring to read.

If the 31st perfect number seems big, it's only a peanut compared to the 39th perfect number which has about 8,200,000 digits and would fill more than SIXTY books like this.

EVEN BETTER!

Perfect number facts

- Write down any perfect number and then write out all its factors. (So if your perfect number is 6, you write out 6, 3, 2, 1.) Make them all into fractions by putting "1" over each number. Add them all up ... and the answer is always 2!
  With 6 you get: $\frac{1}{6} + \frac{1}{1} + \frac{1}{2} + \frac{1}{3} = 2$
  If you try it with the number 28 you get:
  $\frac{1}{1} + \frac{1}{2} + \frac{1}{4} + \frac{1}{7} + \frac{1}{14} + \frac{1}{28} = 2$
  If you try it with the number 33,550,336 you get a headache.
- All perfect numbers are triangular.
- Apart from 6, all perfect numbers are a list of odd cubes added up. In other words $28 = 1^3 + 3^3$ and $496 = 1^3 + 3^3 + 5^3 + 7^3$. We even checked 33,550,336 and found it was $1^3 + 3^3 + 5^3 + ...$ and so on all the way up to ... $+ 127^3$.
- They all seem to end in 6 or 8
- If you subtract 1 from any perfect number (except 6), it will divide by 9.
- They are useless.

145

Your first chance to be famous for ever

Every so often in a Murderous Maths book, you get a chance to be famous for ever, and to prove it soon you'll be reading about a 16-year-old whose name will *never* be forgotten by mathematicans. This chapter will give you not just one but TWO chances.

Here's the first chance – can you find a perfect number that *doesn't* come from Euclid's formula? If you manage it you'll still be famous when people are living on the moon! (Maybe there's a nice little perfect number waiting for you that everybody else has missed so far.)

What would be even better is if you could find a perfect number that is ODD, because so far the Mathsie people have only found even perfect numbers, and they are all getting a bit bored. If you find an odd one, then you'll be famous long after people are living on Mars and nipping off to distant galaxies for their holidays.

WELL AN ODD ONE WOULD BE FABULOUS BUT ANY ONE WOULD DO!

HINT: as this will be quite a murderous job, here's a clue before you start looking – all the odd numbers up to 10^{300} have already been checked to death, so start looking at bigger numbers than that. (By the way 10^{300} is the same as a 1 with 300 zeros after it. So what are you waiting for? Get looking.)

Defective and excessive numbers

A "defective" or "deficient" number means that its factors add up to less than the number. 21 is very defective because its only factors (apart from 21 itself) are 1, 3, and 7 so they only add up to 11. The most defective numbers are prime numbers because all prime numbers only have a factor of 1. A lonely little 1 on its own only adds up to 1. Sad, isn't it?

You can also have "excessive" or "abundant" numbers whose factors add up to more than the number. The number 30 has factors 1, 2, 3, 5, 6, 10 and 15 which all add up to 42.

154,345,556,085,770,649,600 is worth a mention here. If you add up all its divisors you get 926,073,336,514,623,897,600 which is exactly *6 times* the number itself.

If you want to be really keen, you can also have *slightly defective numbers*. These are numbers whose factors add up to one less than themselves. An example is 8, because the factors are $1+2+4$ which total 7. Funnily enough, any power of 2 is slightly defective. For example, $2^7 = 128$. The factors of 128 are 1, 2, 4, 8, 16, 32, 64 and if you add them up you get 127.

Your second chance to be famous for ever

As we just saw, slightly defective numbers have factors that add up to one less than the number, and so obviously *slightly excessive numbers* are numbers whose factors add up to one more than the number itself. There's just one tiny problem – nobody has found any sightly excessive numbers yet! However, the Pure Mathematicians are kicking themselves raw because they cannot prove that there aren't any, so if you could find one they would be terribly grateful to you. It goes without saying that they would all queue up to have their photo taken with you and they would send you strange Christmas cards with unreadable signatures for ever.

Numbers in love

Can you imagine the thrills and fireworks that Pure Mathematicians felt when they discovered 137,438,691,328 and 2,305,843,008,139,952,128 were the 7th and 8th perfect numbers? Some of them went completely nutty and celebrated with THREE sugars in their tea, they stayed up until well past 9 o'clock and rumour has it that one of them even tucked his shirt in. The trouble is that such wild animal behaviour makes you suspect that they don't have room in their souls for normal human emotions. Well you'd be wrong because given the right circumstances they can get quite gooey...

148

220 and 284 are called "amicable" or "friendly" numbers because their factors add up to each other. People thought this was the only pair for thousands of years until 1636 when that French Monsieur Fermat found another pair: 17,296 and 18,416. He started a trend and soon all the top brains were finding bigger and bigger pairs of friendly numbers.

Meet a 16-year-old who IS famous for ever!
The really neat part about the friendly number story is that everybody was looking for new friendly numbers in the tens and hundreds of thousands. But all of a sudden in 1867 a 16-year-old Italian called Nicolo Pananini turned up a much smaller pair of friendly numbers that everybody else had missed: 1,184 and 1,210. Just when the experts thought they knew it all – suddenly they looked a bit daft! Be honest, how many 16-year-olds today do you think will have their names mentioned in new books in 140 years' time?

CHAPTER NINE

Welcome to the weird world of nine.

9

It looks just like a normal number doesn't it? Well don't be fooled, because of all the numbers, nine is probably the most mysterious. Stand by to be amazed as nine demonstrates some strange abilities then goes on to help you perform some mind-defying tricks!

The three tricks of the nine times table

$9 \times 1 = 09$
$9 \times 2 = 18$
$9 \times 3 = 27$
$9 \times 4 = 36$
$9 \times 5 = 45$
$9 \times 6 = 54$
$9 \times 7 = 63$
$9 \times 8 = 72$
$9 \times 9 = 81$
$9 \times 10 = 90$

TENS   UNITS

AMAZING!

Trick 1

Have a look down the units column of the answers. Can you see how the units go 9, 8, 7, 6, 5, 4, 3, 2, 1, 0? Now look down the tens column and you'll see it goes 0, 1, 2, 3, 4, 5, 6, 7, 8, 9. Neat, isn't it? However, there's something even better about this table that

we didn't know until a 12-year-old Murderous Maths
fan called Tom Johnson from Yorkshire told us...

091827364554637281 90

GASP! WHAT GENIUS!

IF YOU WRITE OUT ALL THE ANSWERS IN A LINE, IT'S THE SAME FORWARDS AS BACKWARDS!

TOM JOHNSON

Trick 2
Pick two different two-digit numbers — but the
digits of each number must add to the same total.
(So you could have 83 and 29 because $8 + 3 = 11$ and
$2 + 9 = 11$.) Take the smaller from the bigger one.
The answer always appears on the 9 times table! In
this case $83 - 29 = 54$.

Trick 3 (when calculators can show remainders)
- Get a calculator and push any single number
  from 1 to 8
- Push $\div 9 =$
- The screen fills with the number you first
  pushed!

This trick amuses very small children, parrots,
intelligent pond life and daytime TV presenters, but
actually it's not quite as pointless as it seems. As we
know, calculators are immensely silly when it comes
to division because if there is a remainder they don't
usually tell you what it is, or convert it into a nice
fraction for you. However, there is one exception — a
calculator can tell you what the reminder is if you

are dividing by nine! Put in any big number you like, e.g. 517, and divide it by 9, you get 57·444444. The number before the decimal point is the answer, and the digits after the decimal point all tell you what the remainder is. In other words 9 into 517 goes 57 times with a remainder of 4. This works if you are dividing 9 into any number. If you try the next number up (which is 518) and divide it by nine you get 57·55555, in other words the answer is now 57 with a remainder of 5 which is what you would expect.

So much for strange abilities of the number 9, but now it's…

Put on your glitter jacket, cue the music, fire up the lights, throw open the curtains and leap on to that stage. You are going to knock 'em dead!

First of all you need an audience volunteer, so you go out and grab Malcolm. As you bring him up on stage there is a polite round of applause from everybody else because they are SO relieved you didn't pick on them. Poor Malcolm! His big soft head isn't going to know what's hit it.

(By the way, it's a good idea to ask the audience to watch Malcolm's sums very carefully and make sure he gets them right. You could even lend a calculator to one person in the audience so that he or she can act as a "referee".)

The Big Big Number trick

The Missing Number!

This trick starts in the same way as the Big Big Number trick, but if you know about digital roots (see page 109), you can have a much better ending. If you want to be really showbizzy, before you start you can completely hide your eyes and shut yourself away so that you cannot see what Malcolm is doing! (Mind you, make sure you can trust Malcolm to follow your instructions properly and get the sums right.)

As before, get Malcolm to write down any big number, then he has to write it down again with the digits jumbled up. He then has to take the smaller number from the larger one, and tell him to write down the answer. So far so good, but don't mention the fact that this new number will divide by nine, because this is where the trick changes. Let's suppose Malcolm has done the first bit of the trick and got 27801117 as before...

THE SECRET: When Malcolm tells you what his final number is, you just add up the digits and get the digital root. (With practice you can quickly do it in your head.)

- If the digital root of the number Malcolm gives you is 9, then the number he circled was also a 9!
- Otherwise, once you have worked out the digital root, you just subtract it from 9 and the answer will be the digit that Malcolm circled!

In this case, when Malcolm says his final number is 1081277, you add $1+0+8+1+2+7+7$ and get 26. You then add $2+6$ to get a digital root of 8. You then work out $9-8$ which tells you the number Malcolm circled was a "1".

Here's a quick run through of the different stages:

1 Malcolm writes down any big number.

2 He scrambles the digits up and writes down another number.

3 He takes the smaller number from the bigger one.

4 He takes the answer and puts a circle round any digit except 0.

5 He scrambles up the remaining digits of the answer and then tells you what his final number is.

6 You add up the digits of the final number and get the digital root.

7 If the digital root is 9, then you know Malcolm circled a 9. If the root is another number, subtract it from 9 and that tells you what digit Malcolm circled.

Remember – you have no idea what numbers Malcolm started off with, you don't know the answers to his subtractions, you didn't see how he jumbled the digits up, you didn't see what digit he circled and yet you can still get the answer right. This trick is truly awesome!

A Quick Slick trick

- Ask Malcolm to write down any three-digit number – but all the digits must be different. (Let's say he writes 375.)
- Ask him to write it out again but backwards. (So he writes 573.)
- Take the smaller one from the bigger one. $(573 - 375 = 198.)$
- Ask him what the first digit of the answer is. (He says "1")
- You can tell him what the other digit are digits are! (You say "9" and "8".)

This is so easy because it doesn't matter what three-digit number he writes down to start with, there are only nine different answers he can get: 99, 198, 297, 396, 495, 594, 693, 792 and 891.

- If Malcolm says the first digit is "9" then you immediately know that his answer was "99", so you just say his other digit is also a 9. (He might say "0" in which case the answer is also 99.)

- However, if Malcolm says his first digit is a number between 1 and 8, then you know that the middle digit is always 9, and the first and last digits of his answer will add up to nine. Suppose Malcolm says his first digit is "3", then his answer must be 396. (Because $3+6=9$.) It will only take you a nanosecond to work out that his last two digits are 9 and 6.

By the way, if you take Malcolm's answer and reverse it and then add the two together you *always* get 1089. For instance, $396+693=1089$ or $990+099=1089$. And the strange bit is that it doesn't matter what three digit number Malcolm starts with!

The Prediction

Here's a very spooky trick you can do which once again uses your secret weapon – the number nine! However, before you do it you need to practise something simple. Write down a long number such as 670198. Underneath you have to write down the "anti-nine" number, and in this case it would look like this...

$$670198$$
$$329801$$

If you add these two numbers you get 999999 – and that's the secret of how to get the anti-nine number. You just go along the first number and subtract each digit from 9 and write the answer underneath. Here you'll see that the first number on the top was 6, so take that from 9 and you get 3. Next you take 7 from 9 and get 2 and so on. Writing out the "anti-nine number" for any number doesn't take much practice, and when you can do it, you'll be able to perform this very sharp trick!

It's time to go and get Malcolm (if he has recovered from the Missing Number trick) and ask him to write down any six-digit number across the middle of a bit of paper. While he's doing this, you write your prediction.

Next you ask Malcolm to write two more six-digit numbers above his first number. It might end up looking like this:

You now say you're going to put a couple more numbers into the sum. Malcolm will just think they are any old numbers, but the secret is that you put the anti-nines of the top numbers on the bottom.

The faster you can write them out, the more it looks like you're just making them up.

589011
883723
478309 — THE ANTI-NINE OF 589011
410988
116276 — THE ANTI-NINE OF 883723

You then get Malcolm to add all five of the numbers up. You can pretend he's being very slow and even lend him a calculator if you like. Finally:

FINISHED!

NOW TAKE THE PAPER OUT OF YOUR POCKET.

TOTAL = 2478307

GASP!

2478307

CONFIDENT SMIRK

What a complete belter of a trick, eh? But providing you get your anti-nines correct, it's so DEAD SIMPLE. When Malcolm writes down his first number (which in this case was 478309), you subtract 2 and write it down, (so in this case you put 478307). You then put another "2" on the front! That's how 478309 turned into 2478307!

The reason this works is that after Malcolm has written down his first number, all that happens is that two lots of 999999 get added to it. This is the same as adding 2000000 and taking away 2! Suppose Malcolm's first number was 978501, your anti-nines can force the answer to be 2978499, regardless of what other numbers he picks afterwards.

If you are brave, you can do this trick using seven- or eight-digit numbers (or even more!). Just do the same thing when you write out the prediction – subtract 2 from Malcolm's first number, and put an extra "2" on the front! If the first number is 86936742, the "prediction" will be 286936740.

Two 9 and 1089 facts
We've already seen the number 1089 turn up in this book a couple of times and nobody will blame you if you're getting rather fond of it. Just for you then, here are yet two more of the odd things it does:

- $1089 \times 9 = 9801$ which is 1089 backwards! (This also works with 10989 or 109989 or 1099989...)
- $1 \div 1089 = 0.000918273645546372819...$

As soon as you realize where we've seen that long string of digits before, you'll see why it gets an award!

The curse of "9"
Finally, here's an odd fact that has nothing to do with maths, but it's interesting all the same:

In a pack of cards, the nine of diamonds used to be called "the curse of Scotland"! This is probably because of one of the nastiest episodes in Scottish history – The Massacre of Glencoe – was organized

162

by the Earl of Stair, whose coat of arms had nine diamond shapes on it. For many years afterwards card games were being invented in which the nine of diamonds had a special significance and when it turned up it usually meant something bad.

THE NIGHT OF MAD AND GHOSTLY NUMBERS

It's breakfast time in Numberworld. The sun shines, the birds tweet and $17 + 9 = 26$ so everything is nice and normal.

Lunchtime approaches, fluffy white clouds drift across the sky, and $23 - 16 = 7$. If you're feeling crazy, you could swap the sum round and get $16 - 23 = -7$. Gosh! You get a *minus* 7 as the answer but so what? For fun you decide to add 8 to it. $-7 + 8 = 1$. There now, nothing to be afraid of, was there?

Teatime, your muffins are toasting by the fire and $5 \times 7 = 35$. It's so reassuring to see nice chunky numbers behaving normally.

The evening draws in, so close the curtains and click the light on. There's a whispering sound outside. Probably just a breeze getting up. Who knows? Who cares? At least there's no mystery with numbers. $20 \div 5 = 4$. You can't argue with that.

You do another: $7 \div 8$ … there's a tapping on the window! Relax – it's a branch from the old beech tree being blown about by the wind. Don't bother looking, concentrate on $7 \div 8$ instead. But your answer refuses to form into a nice solid chunky number! At least you can make it into a fraction $\frac{7}{8}$. Not quite as pleasing as having one single number as the answer, but there again it's just two whole numbers on top of each other. Maybe if you put the sum into the calculator it'll turn into something nice. Click click click and you get 0·875. That's OK. Decimal points are cool and 875 looks nice and tidy.

The noise at the window – surely that was something scratching? No – you're letting your imagination run away. Calm your mind with some good reliable sums that give down-to-earth answers. You try $9 \div 11$. Of course it makes $\frac{9}{11}$ but you can't resist reaching for the calculator to see what it conjures up.

A scream outside.

What was that? It was a cat, definitely a cat. It *must* have been a cat, after all what else would scream like that? Gosh that wind is really whipping up now. The curtains are trembling slightly. Ignore it, grab the calculator, enter nine divide by eleven equals 0·818181818181818... Surely not! How can two nice normal little numbers produce this monster? It must be a mistake. Push cancel then try again.

$9 \div 11 = 0.818181818181818...$

No mistake. The calculator screen stares at you unblinking. What has happened? *Your meddling experiments in Numberworld have created an uncontrollable decimal which stretches way beyond the confines of the calculator screen!*

Your mind battles to comprehend this line of digits that goes on for ever. Sure, you know it starts with 0·81 but you must not attempt to see the other end. If you wrote this number out in a long line and then ran along it clearing over 1,000 digits with each step, you would have died of old age long before you got halfway.

In a cold sweat you turn all the lights up and pace the room. Outside the wind drops to a quiet moan. You must get a grip on yourself. Look again at the calculator: it's just a row of eights and ones. So the last digit is either an 8 or a 1. The number can stretch as far as it likes but there's no big mystery about it. Hah! Division can't scare you, and to prove it you try another: $22 \div 26$ which makes $\frac{22}{26}$. No worries, you could just leave it and go to bed. But hey, just to show you're cool, you use a trick from *The Mean and Vulgar Bits*. You cancel it down by dividing top and bottom by 2. You get $\frac{11}{13}$. That's it, no more for tonight.

PHEW!

You prepare to leave the room, when from behind you hear a clattering sound. Your calculator has slipped to the floor. Funny — you don't remember knocking into it. You pick it up and check it. It seems OK, but what's that on the screen? The number 11. The buttons must have got pushed as it fell. It's almost as if the calculator has started to work out the fraction itself. You laugh lightly. Well, why not finish the job? After all numbers can't hurt you. $11 \div 13$ equals 0·84615384615384615…

You recoil in horror. What is this fearsome numerical abomination? You cannot tear your eyes away – and yet as you look you realize that it's quite tame. The digits 846153 just keep repeating and repeating. It's no worse than 0·818181818.

Rational numbers

You don't have to worry that the numbers go on for ever, at least you know what they are. That's because any fraction made of two nice solid whole numbers is *rational*. Sometimes fractions such as $\frac{2}{3}$ are called ratios, and that's where the word *ratio*nal comes from. It doesn't matter which two whole numbers you pick to make your fraction, when you make it into a decimal you'll either get a simple answer or a set of digits that keep repeating. Suddenly you realize that you can control numbers, even when they arrive in infinite chains. It feels good.

As the rain starts to lash against the window, you consider this interesting question:

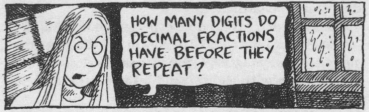

HOW MANY DIGITS DO DECIMAL FRACTIONS HAVE BEFORE THEY REPEAT?

It depends on the number you're dividing by.
- If you divide by 3 there will only be 1 digit that repeats because $1 \div 3 = 0·33333...$
- If you divide by 11 there will be two digits that repeat: $1 \div 11 = 0·09\ 09\ 09\ 09...$ (We've put gaps in to show where the repeat comes)

- If you divide by 41 there are five digits that repeat: $1 \div 41 = 0 \cdot 02439\ 02439\ 02439$ ...
- If you divide by 17 there are a whopping great *sixteen* digits that repeat themselves: $1 \div 17 = 0 \cdot 0588235294117647\ 0588235294117647$ ...

WHAT IS THE BIGGEST NUMBER OF DIGITS YOU CAN HAVE BEFORE REPEATING?

The absolute maximum number of repeating digits is one less than the dividing number. Dividing by 17 creates the maximum because you get 16 digits that repeat. Only prime numbers can create the maximum number of repeating digits, and even then most of them don't bother. (41 is a prime, but it only creates 5 repeating digits.) The number 97 is rather fine because it uses the maximum – in other words $1 \div 97$ produces a string of 96 digits before they start repeating!

The number 7 gives some especially odd results. If you work out 1/7, 2/7, 3/7, 4/7, 5/7 or 6/7 the repeating digits are always 142857. You just need to know which digit to start with e.g. $4/7 = 0 \cdot 57\ 142857\ 142857$...

How to tame rational numbers
Although it's a bit scary having numbers so long that you can't see the end, you can invent sums that get rid of the billions and billions of digits that go on for ever! Think about this:

$1/11 = 0 \cdot 090909090909$.... and so on

Because there are *two* repeating digits, you divide this number by 100 (which is a 1 with *two* zeros). You get $1/1100 = 0.000909090909...$

The good bit is that both these numbers have a never-ending chain of 09090909... which stretches away around the world and off into space. BUT if you work out $1/11 - 1/1100$ in decimals you get:

0·09090909...

− 0·00090909...

= 0·09

You get an exact answer of 0·09. You've tamed the infinite chain!

(By the way, if you work out $1/11 - 1/1100$ in normal fractions you get 99/1100 which you now know is exactly equal to 0·09.)

Because 1/41 has five repeating digits, you need to work out that $1/4100000 = 0.00000\ 02439\ 02439....$ Then when you work out $1/41 - 1/4100000$ you find that $\frac{99999}{4100000}$ equals exactly 0·02439.

So there you are. It doesn't matter what spooky effects numbers try to conjure up to scare you, there's a nice rational explanation for everything. Go to bed, sleep well and just don't worry about square roots.

Don't worry. After all you know what square roots are, don't you? You read about them on page 43 remember? Just to put your mind at rest, here's how to deal with the square root of 4: $\sqrt{4} = 2$. Cute, isn't it?

Now go to sleep...

...and don't think about the square root of 5.

It's the number which you multiply by itself to make five. Obviously it's bigger than 2 because $2 \times 2 = 4$. And it's smaller than 3 because $3 \times 3 = 9$. So the square root of 5 is somewhere in between 2 and 3. But don't worry about it.

No. You'll find that $(2\frac{1}{2})^2 = 6\frac{1}{4}$ so it's a bit big.

Sorry. $(2\frac{1}{4})^2 = 5\frac{1}{16}$ or $5 \cdot 0625$ so it's still a bit too big. Night night.

Er... $(2\frac{1}{5})^2$ makes 4·84 so it's too small. Of course, if you *really* want to know, your calculator button has a $\sqrt{}$ button on it, but you left it downstairs, didn't you? But don't go and get it now, wait until the morning!

It's no good. You *have* to know the awful truth. Outside an angry storm is thrashing the trees and buildings. With a trembling hand you reach for the light switch. Click. Nothing. You find your torch – curses! Why didn't you get new batteries? The bulb flickers sadly as your naked feet find their way downstairs. A ray of moonlight cuts through a chink in the curtains and catches the calculator on the edge of the table. A moment's hesitation then you grab it and hurriedly push the 5. Your finger hovers over the mysterious $\sqrt{}$. It's not too late to go back, but *no* you've come this far. Your finger stabs the button that will take you into the unknown...

There's your answer! Millions of digits that go on for ever in a pattern that never repeats. It makes no sense, it's mad, it defies logic, it … it's **irrational**.

Irrational numbers

You can never write down irrational numbers exactly, either as a normal fraction or as a decimal with repeating digits. It's easy to make irrational numbers, all you do is find the square root of any number that isn't a perfect square. Of the numbers under 10, only 1, 4, and 9 are perfect squares. If you worked out the square roots of 2, 3, 5, 6, 7 or 8, they would all be irrational.

There are lots of other roots you can get from numbers. After square roots comes cube roots which are easy enough: two cubed $= 2^3 = 2 \times 2 \times 2 = 8$. This means that the cube root of 8 is 2. However, the cube root of 9 is 2·08008382305190411… The fact that the square root of 9 is rational doesn't stop the cube root of 9 being completely mad.

So there you are in the middle of the night with an utterly demented square root thrashing around the room and knocking all your framed photographs off the grand piano. How do you get rid if it, especially when it runs into millions of digits that have never ever been calculated? You need help…

Obviously the whole point of $\sqrt{5}$ is that $\sqrt{5} \times \sqrt{5} = 5$ so you can get rid of square roots just by squaring them! And if you cube a cube root, you can get rid of it too. So you can go to bed now knowing that irrational numbers can be controlled even if you don't know exactly what they are.

SLEEP WELL. IRRATIONAL NUMBERS ARE NO THREAT TO US.

JUST SO LONG AS THEY AREN'T TRANSCENDENTAL!

The most famous transcendental number

It starts with 3·141592653 ... and as any Murderous Maths fan will know, this is usually written as π which is pronounced "pi". If you draw any circle then measure it round the outside and divide by the diameter, this is the number you get. What makes a transcendental number like π different from your common little irrational numbers is that you can

SIMPLIFY YOURSELF! NEVER!

double it, square it, cube it, root it, boil it up with peas and carrots or drive over it with a steamroller, but you'll *still* get an infinite line of digits that go on for ever in no recognizable pattern. (At least that's what everybody thinks. That's one of the beauties of transcendental numbers, it's really hard to tell if they *are* transcendental.)

π has been a source of mystery for thousands of years because it turns up so often, and yet nobody actually knows exactly what it is! You'll find quite a bit more about π in other Murderous Maths books, but we've saved some of the most gloriously useless facts for this book, so here they come:

● Most people only need to use approximate values including 3·14 or $3\frac{1}{7}$. The ancient Greeks and the Egyptians all used very close values for π when they were designing buildings and doing sums. However, the Romans often couldn't be bothered. They didn't even use $3\frac{1}{7}$, instead they would use $3\frac{1}{8}$ because it was easier. On some jobs they even used π = 4 . It's amazing that their posh temples and statues didn't all collapse straight away.

● So far computers have calculated well over 200,000,000,000 digits of π. If you want to get a computer to work out even more digits, do bear in mind one little problem – how do you know your new digits are correct? The answer is that you have to have a second computer calculating π using a completely different method, and then make sure they get exactly the same digits. Hint: if you are going to check the billions of digits are the same for both answers, don't try and do it yourself. Use a third computer.

- There's a π fan club! If you want to join you have to learn the first 100 digits off by heart. They are: 3·141592653 5897932384 6264338327 9502884197 1693993751 0582097494 4592307816 4062862089 9862803482 5342117067

  (Warning! Some people insist that you have to know the first 100 *decimal* digits which means that the first "3" doesn't count and you'll need to know one more digit at the end. Just so's you know, the next digit is 9. Then 8. Then 2 then 1480865 1328230664 7093844609 5505822317 253 ... arghhhh! It's addictive.)

- Knowing 100 digits is peanuts. Hiroyuki Goto (age 21) of Japan correctly recited the first 42,195 digits of π in 9 hours. Even a 12-year-old called Zhang Zhuo from China managed to recite the first 4,000 digits in 25 minutes, which means he had to say them at the rate of almost *three digits every second*! He didn't just need a massive memory, he needed a very tough mouth. It would have been like reading this whole chapter out loud in 25 minutes. Go on, try it!

- The biggest π fan ever must have been the German mathematician Ludolph van Ceulen. He died in 1610 having spent most of his life working out the first 35 digits of π by investigating a shape with over 32,000,000,000 sides. The sad bit is that soon after he died all sorts of people suddenly hit upon much easier ways of doing it!

However, some Germans still call π the "Ludolphian" number after him. By the way, Ludolph, if you're up there looking down and reading this book over somebody's shoulder, we've got MASSIVE respect for you. Yo.

- There are 360° in a circle, and if you look at the 359th, 360th and 361st digits of π you get 3 6 0.

- There's a π dance! Amazing as it might seem, we found this out from no lesser a person than Dr Hugh Hunt of Cambridge University which is where all the mega brainy people go. He told us that when he was growing up in Australia, he and his school mates would stand in a long line and each person would pretend there was a giant calculator on the floor in front of them. When the music started they would step on the pretend keys as if they were entering the digits 3·141592653...

All of them would have their feet moving to the beat in exactly the same pattern which looked utterly mysterious to anyone who didn't know what they were doing. So the next time you want to really go crazy and boogie on down, you know what to do. If it's good enough for top Cambridge academics, it's good enough for us.

- If you see π typed out in one long continuous line, count your way along to the 53,217,681,704th digit (this will be about 67,000 miles along from the first "3"). This digit is a 0 which is then followed by 1, 2, 3, 4, 5, 6, 7, 8, 9 and then another 0. It's the first time these digits appear in sequence.
- There's a group of people who think that if you work out billions of billions of billions of digits of π you might discover a secret message from a parallel civilization co-inhabiting our universe. And there's another group of people who think the first group are totally potty.

The second most famous transcendental number 2·718281828459045... which is otherwise known by the letter: e.

e is "the base of natural logarithms". Wahey! Doesn't that sound interesting? We'll get round to explaining it in the 428th Murderous Maths book. That's a promise, so order your copy now to avoid disappointment.

Although e is used for some of the most murderous maths invented, the good thing about e is that you can cook one up yourself. All you need is a calculator that can do high powers so look for a button marked x^y.

This is the formula to use:

$e = (1 + \frac{1}{x})^x$ and you have to put in the very biggest value for x that you can.

Urgh! Actually it isn't quite as unfriendly as it looks. Here's what to do:

- To start, try replacing the "x" in the formula with 10. You get:
  $e = (1 + \frac{1}{10})^{10}$

- When you do formulas you always work out the bits inside the brackets first, and the reason we chose x to be 10 is that $\frac{1}{10}$ becomes 0·1. Therefore the bit in the brackets is just $(1 + \frac{1}{10}) = 1·1$.

- Finally you just need to grab your calculator and work out $(1·1)^{10}$. To do that you push these buttons: 1·1 x^y 10 = and the answer should be something like 2·5937.

This isn't too far away from the exact value for e. However, if you want to get an even more accurate value, replace the "x" with 100. The bit inside the brackets becomes: $1 + \frac{1}{100} = 1·01$ so you then finish by pushing these buttons: 1·01 x^y 100 = and the answer will be 2·7048 which is closer.

Now try replacing the x with 1000, or 10,000 or 100,000! The answer will get closer and closer to e. There's just one small problem. To get the *exact* value of e you have to replace x with INFINITY!

SO WHAT DOES 'e' ACTUALLY DO?

e does all sorts of odd things, and one of the most interesting is that it's used by huge banks to calculate the growth of *money*. Banks are so happy when you leave your cash with them that they give you back a bit more money than you put in. By the way, this next bit is clever stuff so we recommend you read it out loud. Even if you don't quite understand it, you'll sound brilliant.

The tale of three bank managers
Suppose you have £1 and want to put it in a bank. You have a choice of three extremely kind bank managers:

AFTER EVERY 100 DAYS I'LL GIVE YOU AN EXTRA £1 FOR EVERY £1 YOU ALREADY HAVE IN THE BANK.

MR MIDAS

AFTER EVERY 50 DAYS I'LL GIVE YOU AN EXTRA 50p FOR EVERY £1 YOU ALREADY HAVE IN THE BANK.

MRS SCROOGE

AFTER EVERY 10 DAYS I'LL GIVE YOU AN EXTRA 10p FOR EVERY £1 YOU ALREADY HAVE IN THE BANK.

MR GENEVA

At first glance it looks like they are all offering the same deal, but a bit of murderous maths will quickly show you where you should put your money!

Let's see how much money you'll finish with after 100 days in each bank.

- On the 100th day Mr Midas gives you an extra £1 for every £1 you already have in the bank, so you'll have an extra £1 plus your original £1 making £2.

- On the 50th day Mrs Scrooge gives you an extra 50p for every £1 you have in the bank, so that's $1 \times 50p = 50p$. Add this to the £1 you've already got and you'll end up with £1·50. But then on the 100th day she's again going to give you 50p for every pound in the bank, and this time you've got £1·50 already there! So you get an extra $1·5 \times 50p = 75p$. If you add this to the £1·50 you already have, you'll find that after 100 days you'll end up with £2·25.

- On the 10th day Mr Geneva gives you an extra 10p for every £1, so you end up with an extra $1 \times 10p = 10p$ making your total into £1·10. On the 20th day he gives you $1·1 \times 10p = 11p$ so your total becomes $£1·10 + 11p = £1·21$. On the 30th day you'll finish with a total of £1·33, on the 40th day you'll have £1·46 ... and so on until the 100th day when you end up with £2·58.

- Now suppose you find a fourth bank manager who gives you 1p for every £1 you have in the bank *every day*. On the 100th day you'll end up with £2·70.

- And if you find a fifth bank manager who checks your account ten times every day, and each time gives you $\frac{1}{10}$th of a penny for every £1 you have in the bank ... at the end of the 100th day you'll have very close to £ e in the bank!

181

Even if you don't quite understand the sums, there is one extremely important point that all loyal Murderous Maths readers should learn from this. If you ever discover a bank manager who gives away money as quickly as Mr Geneva, grab hold of him, cling on tight and send us an urgent message saying you've got him. And whatever you do, don't let him go until we get there.

e also has a strange habit of turning up in the most unexpected places, but the only one that any of us have the slightest chance of understanding is this...

Loads of blokes have gone to the pool, but just as they get their kit off they realize that someone has pinched *all* their swimming trunks. Luckily the attendant spots Veronica Gumfloss giggling away in the spectators gallery clutching a huge bag of clothing and a pair of binoculars. Just as the attendant takes the bag into the men's changing room, there is a power cut

and the whole place goes completely dark. Each bloke grabs a pair of trunks and pulls them on. The probability that they *all* have the wrong trunks on is about 1/*e* which is 0·3679. In other words if

Veronica tries it 3 times, you should expect them all to have the wrong trunks on at least once.

There are lots of other transcendental numbers, but now it's time to see if we can encounter something *really* spooky...

The ghostly number

The moon has risen, the wind has dropped, and you've finally convinced yourself that no harm can come from massive numbers that stretch into infinity. After all, you can always round them off and tidy them up. π becomes 3·14 and if you ever needed to use e then 2·718 should satisfy anyone. You could mark these values on a ruler, and if the ruler was extended beyond the "0" you could even mark negative numbers such as $-e$.

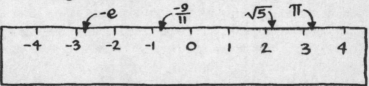

You chuckle as you think back to your nightmares of irrational numbers. It all seems rather petty now. Yawning gently, you make one last effort to get everything straight in your head. $1^2 = 1$ and so $\sqrt{1} = 1$ is easy enough. So does $(-1)^2$ make -1? Sadly no...

183

That's right. In fact $\sqrt{1}$ can be $+1$ *or* -1. You can even write this with the special plus-or-minus sign: $\sqrt{1} = \pm 1$ Now there's a nice little thought to take back up to bed with you. But as you pass the mirror, you shiver as a question forms in your mind:

It can't be! Your reflection is trying to tell you something ... but how can that be? The image in the mirror isn't real. You can't touch it, you can't walk round it – it's purely imaginary. And yet it is holding up the answer to the square root of minus one. This is known as the number "*i*" because i stands for *imaginary*!

Surely it's just a trick of the light, but the worst is yet to come...

i might be imaginary, but like any self-respecting ghost, it exists!

As weird as it seems, $i = \sqrt{-1}$ is one of the coolest tricks in maths. As long as you know that $i \times i = -1$ then you can use it to describe any negative square root. For example $\sqrt{-9} = 3i$ because $3i \times 3i = -9$. Engineers use it a lot when they design things like electric generators, although instead of the letter *i* they tend to use the letter *j*. It makes things a bit clearer because engineers always have rotten handwriting. (And here's a message to any offended engineers: don't write in and complain to us because we won't be able to read it.)

So where do you think you'd mark the ghostly number *i* on your ruler? You know it isn't the same as 1 or -1, and you can't even mark it at the "0" because $0 \times 0 = 0$.

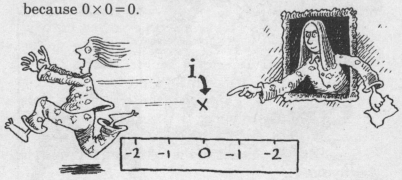

Yes, in the same way that ghosts float and can walk through walls without touching them, the number *i* floats above the ruler without touching it! How? Why? We'll go into it another time, you've had enough for one night.

Sunrise and the elegant formula

As the night sky pales into dawn, you're amazed to think of the nightmares you conjured from a few innocent digits. Irrational powers, infinite transcendentals, imaginary roots ... and then suddenly in the golden glow of the rising sun it all makes sense. It's so simple, so pure, so blazingly obvious. It's this: $e^{i\pi} + 1 = 0$

Well, maybe you didn't realize this but that genius we've already met called Euler did. It looks complicated, but in the Murderous Maths testing lab we can prove that when you think about $e^{i\pi}$ and then add 1 you end up with nothing.

START WITH e WHICH IS 2.718...

WILLING VOLUNTEER

RAISE IT TO THE POWER OF THE SQUARE ROOT OF MINUS 1...

THE END OF THE END

We've come a long way since the beginning of this book, but now we're about to reach into the deep number zone. We've already seen a few numbers in the billions and trillions but it's time for the massive leap towards infinity. It's so big that you can hurt yourself if you try to imagine it – but luckily infinity has a teeny little sign to make life easier: ∞.

So let's go back to where we came in. You'll remember Tezza Goldbars has infinity full seats and needs to sit one more person down. So long as you agree that the number infinity goes on for ever without ending then here's the solution...

The person on seat number 1 moves to seat number 2. The person on seat 2 moves to seat 3, and so on. Everybody moves up one seat – and why not? If there are infinity seats then nobody will fall off the far end! This leaves seat number 1 empty and the singer's mother can sit down.

The amazing thing is that in the end there will be infinity *plus 1* people sitting on infinity seats. So infinity = infinity + 1. But it gets worse...

"Phew," said Tezza to Shakk. "Now the concert can start."

"Er ... not quite!" said Shakk as a giant wormhole opened behind him. "It seems that infinity more life forms have arrived from the anti-universe and they want seats too!"

"But we already have infinity full seats!" wailed Tezza. "What do we do?"

There is an answer!

Everybody looks at their seat number and multiplies it by 2. Then they go and sit on the seat with the new number. So the person on seat 1 goes to 2, the person on seat 2 goes to 4 and so on. And why not? There are an infinity of even numbers, so the infinity people should all fit on nicely. And that leaves an infinity of odd-numbered seats all ready for the infinity of anti-universe visitors.

In terms of sums: $2 \times \text{infinity} = \text{infinity}$.

"And there's just one more thing," said Shakk.

"WHAT?" wept Tezza.

"We've only got three toilets."

To his amazement Tezza burst out laughing.

"Relax, Shakk," she smiled. "Remember this is a pop concert and if there's one thing I know about pop concerts, there's *never* enough toilets."

THE FINAL JUDGEMENT

While this book was being put together, all sorts of Murderous Maths fans from all over the world voted for their top three Pathetically Useless Facts. They are so fabulous that we've been saving them up especially for you, but now here they come...

2 is the only number that gives the same result added to itself as it does times by itself.

To multiply 10,112,359,550,561,797,752,808,988, 764,044,943,820,224,719 by 9 you just move the 9 at the very end up to the front. It's the only number that does this.

Finally before we go, we'd like to thank you for joining us in our *Numbers* book and remind you that if you've understood it then you really do hold the Key to the Universe! And now, until we see you again we leave you with what was easily voted to be the absolute runaway undisputed heavyweight MOST PATHETIC AND USELESS FACT IN MATHS...